400
B

Goodnight Children Everywhere

Richard Nelson's plays include *The General from America* (RSC), *New England* (RSC, Manhattan Theatre Club), *Misha's Party* (co-written with Alexander Gelman for the Royal Shakespeare Company and the Moscow Art Theatre), *Colombus and the Discovery of Japan* (RSC), *Two Shakespearean Actors* (RSC, Lincoln Center Theatre), *Some Americans Abroad* (RSC, Lincoln Center Theatre), *Sensibility and Sense* (American Playhouse Television), *Principia Scriptoriae* (RSC, Manhattan Theatre Club), *Between East and West*, *Life Sentences*, *The Return of Pinocchio*, *Rip Van Winkle or The Works*, *The Vienna Notes* and *An American Comedy*. Radio plays include *Languages Spoken Here* (BBC Radio 3), *Eating Words* (Radio 4 and the World Service), *Roots in Water* (Radio 3), *Advice to Eastern Europe* (Radio 4) and *The American Wife* (Radio 3). He has written a television play, *End of a Sentence* (American Playhouse), a film, *Ethan Frome*, and a children's play, *Kenneth's First Play* (with Colin Chambers). Among his awards are the prestigious Lila Wallace Reader's Digest Award in 1991, a London *Time Out* award, two Obies, two Giles Cooper Awards, a Guggenheim Fellowship, two Rockefeller playwriting grants and two National Endowment for the Arts playwriting fellowships. He is an Honorary Associate Artist of the RSC.

Making Plays: The Writer–Director Relationship in the Theatre Today, co-written by David Jones and edited by Colin Chambers, was published in 1995 by Faber and Faber.

D0107057

by the same author

plays
THE GENERAL FROM AMERICA
NEW ENGLAND
SENSIBILITY AND SENSE
SOME AMERICANS ABROAD
TWO SHAKESPEAREAN ACTORS
PRINCIPIA SCRIPTORIAE
BETWEEN EAST AND WEST
COLUMBUS AND THE DISCOVERY OF JAPAN
MISHA'S PARTY (with Alexander Gelman)
LIFE SENTENCES

non-fiction
MAKING PLAYS: THE WRITER–DIRECTOR RELATIONSHIP IN THE
THEATRE TODAY (with David Jones, edited by Colin Chambers)

RICHARD NELSON

Goodnight Children
Everywhere

faber and faber
LONDON · BOSTON

First published in 1977
by Faber and Faber Limited
3 Queen Square London WC1N 3AU

Typeset by Faber and Faber Ltd
Printed in England by Mackays of Chatham plc, Chatham, Kent

All rights reserved

© Richard Nelson, 1997
Introduction © Colin Chambers, 1997

Richard Nelson is hereby identified as author of this
work in accordance with Section 77 of the Copyright,
Designs and Patents Act 1988.

All rights whatsoever in this work are strictly reserved. Applications for
permission for any use whatsoever including performance rights must be
made in advance, prior to any such proposed use, to Macnaughton Lord
Representation, 200 Fulham Road, London SW10 9PN (for UK), or to
William Morris Agency, 1325 Sixth Avenue, New York, NY 10019. No
performance may be given unless a licence has first been obtained.

Lyrics from 'Goodnight Children Everywhere', written by Harry Phillips
and Gaby Rogers, published by Cecil Lennox Ltd. for the world, reprinted
by kind permission of Cecil Lennox Ltd., a Kassner Group Company,
Exmouth House, 11 Pine Street, London EC1R 0JH. All rights reserved.
Lyrics from 'Bells of St Mary' reprinted by permission.

*This book is sold subject to the condition that it shall not, by way of trade
or otherwise, be lent, resold, hired out or otherwise circulated without the
publisher's prior consent in any form of binding or cover other than that
in which it is published and without a similar condition including
this condition being imposed on the subsequent purchaser.*

A CIP record for this book
is available from the British Library

ISBN 0-571-19430-3

2 4 6 8 10 9 7 5 3

For Zoe and Jocelyn

Introduction

World War II. Bombs are falling. A twelve-year-old boy is
sent away from his home in South London to Canada;
one sister stays at home, the other two are evacuated to
Wales. Five years later, in the spring of 1945, now a
young man, he returns home. His mother and father are
both dead, and his three sisters are waiting anxiously.

Goodnight Children Everywhere, like many of Richard
Nelson's plays, opens against the chaotic backdrop of history, just as his own professional writing career did. Born
half-way through the century in Chicago, Nelson spent a
year in Manchester after graduating from Hamilton
College in New York State and returned to the US in
1973 as the Vietnam war entered its final phase and the
Watergate affair started to unravel. His early work bears
the imprint of contemporary history, beginning in 1975
with *The Killing of Yablonski*, in which a reporter investi-
gates a politically motivated assassination.

With later plays, the historical context broadens – the
American War of Independence in *The General from
America*, the removal of the Jews and the Moors from
15th-century imperial Spain in *Columbus and the
Discovery of Japan* – yet in each case Nelson is writing
about today and uses history, of whichever period, to
chronicle our beliefs, our passions, our confusions with
scrupulous skill and ironic intelligence.

The apparent ease with which he moves through different moments in history is matched by his command of different theatrical forms – the epic *Rip Van Winkle or The
Works*, the expressionistic *Bal* or the domestic *Goodnight
Children Everywhere*, set in a single room in which stage

time is the same as real time; and in several plays the theatrical is itself a vital element of the story. The rivalry between the legendary 19th-century thespians, the American Edwin Forrest and the English William Charles Macready, which led to riots and fatalities, is emblematically as well as realistically represented in *Two Shakespearean Actors* as the audience sees their contrasting versions of *Macbeth* simultaneously, and hilariously; and they end the play together, alone, on a bare stage, chastened yet somehow unified by their common pursuit.

A prolific and varied writer, Nelson is also the author of a screenplay, a television play, the book for a musical and a play for young audiences, as well as a string of radio plays and powerful adaptations from the classic European repertoire of Beaumarchais, Brecht, Chekhov, Erdman, Fo, Goldoni, Molière and Strindberg, all of which have influenced the development of his own craft.

He wrote most of these adaptations while serving as a literary manager in the 1980s in various American theatres. This experience stood him in good stead for the rigours that awaited him as a playwright and added another important dimension to his understanding of his craft, which is captured with surprising good humour in *Making Plays*, the informative book he wrote with the director David Jones on the often troublesome relationship between a writer and a director in the theatre.

In *Goodnight Children Everywhere*, Nelson revisits a constant theme, that of displacement. The returning evacuee has been physically displaced, as have two of his sisters, and Nelson explores what effect this has on the reunited siblings. The displacement in his plays can often be literal like this; in *Between East and West* a Czech couple are trying to refashion their lives in exile in New York. But the displacement is always emotional too and leads to a questioning, of ideology, of ideals, of art, of life's purpose. It can be an alienation from one's self and one's country, or a more general sense of rootlessness, usually thrown into relief by the impact of a distinct cultural difference.

Nelson enjoys exploiting such differences and often places his characters in another country to do so: in *Some Americans Abroad*, a group of American academics are found on the heritage trail in England; in *Misha's Party* (co-written with the Russian playwright Alexander Gelman), an American woman is staying in a Moscow hotel with her granddaughter when a coup is launched and fighting erupts on the streets outside; and in the book for the New York production of the musical *Chess*, cold war competitors Russia and the USA pursue their confrontation across the chequered board.

Beyond a satirical impulse, maybe this desire to dramatize cultural contradictions was sharpened by Nelson's own early lack of recognition in America when, had it not been for his acceptance in Britain through the championing of him by the Royal Shakespeare Company, he might have given up playwriting altogether.

The nation of America is built on such displacement, yet, paradoxically, Nelson was for some time seen there as a European writer. As Nelson's plays began to find their audience in the US, however, the richness of his work became even more evident. When his plays were presented both in Britain and in America, the difference in audience reaction was a testimony to the fertile quality of his texts. There is a music to his plays which, if found, can reveal the many layers of meaning which can rarely be grasped at a first encounter.

In *Goodnight Children Everywhere*, displacement throws the emphasis on to the many meanings of home – home as a country, as a town, as a place where you live, as a room, as a family – but also on to the nature of the close relationships that once, perhaps, were taken for granted. It asks questions that touch us all, such as what it is to be a sister or a brother, a father or a mother, a child, a woman or a man.

Colin Chambers
September 1997

Characters

Peter, 17
Betty, 21, his sister
Ann, 20, his sister
Vi, 19, his sister
Mike, early fifties, married to Ann
Hugh, forties
Rose, 19, Hugh's daughter

Time: Late spring, 1945
Setting: The living-room of a flat in Clapham,
South London

Goodnight Children Everywhere was first performed by the Royal Shakespeare Company at The Other Place, Stratford-upon-Avon, on 4 December 1997. The cast, in order of appearance, was as follows:

Betty Sara Markland
Ann Cathryn Bradshaw
Vi Robin Weaver
Mike Colin McCormack
Peter Simon Scardifield
Hugh Malcolm Scates
Rose Aislinn Mangan

Director Ian Brown
Designer Tim Hatley
Lighting Designer Peter Mumford
Composer Richard Sisson
Sound Martin Slavin
Music Director Michael Tubbs
Company voice work Andrew Wade and Lyn Darnley
Production Manager Benita Wakefield
Costume Supervisor Lucy Roberts

Stage Manager Monica McCabe
Deputy Stage Manager Maddy Grant
Assistant Stage Manager Stephen Cressy

A large flat, Clapham, South London. Late spring, 1945.
    The living-room; chairs, a sofa, two small tables, one with photographs in frames. Three doors: one to the outside hallway and stairs, one to a hall which leads to two bedrooms and the W.C., and one that leads to the kitchen and the third bedroom (Mike and Ann's).
    Ann, 20, five-months pregnant, sits on the sofa, her feet tucked under her, reading a book, or pretending to. Betty, 21, fusses with the table.
    After a pause:

Betty I remember on Peter's eleventh birthday Father turning on the gramophone, setting up chairs in a line, telling us to keep walking, then – grab a chair when he stopped the music. We couldn't stop playing the game. It was hysterically funny, do you remember?

    No response.

There was one less chair, so . . . (*Beat.*) Then it seemed like the very next day Peter was gone.

    Vi, 19, bursts in from one of the bedrooms.

Vi He's here! I just saw them out the window!

    Betty begins to fuss harder, mumbling, 'Oh God, oh my God.' Vi rushes to the door, opens it, listens, closes it.

They're coming up the stairs!

    Vi turns back to the room. She and Betty share a look. Betty stops fussing and goes to her, takes Vi's hand and holds it tightly in hers.

I

Silence. Footsteps. The door opens.
Mike (Ann's husband), 53, enters with Peter, the girls'
17-year-old brother. He carries his suitcase.
Ann has stood at a distance to watch.

Betty Peter! Oh my God, look at him! Look at you!

Betty and Vi rush him, hug him, they can't take their
hands off him. Mike watches with a smile.

(*while hugging Peter with Vi, to Mike*) Was the train late?

Mike (*shakes his head, then*) We missed each other. This
photo you gave me . . . (*Holds up snapshot.*)

Betty (*pulling Peter*) Come in, come in. I've made you
something to eat.

Peter I'm not –.

Betty Mike has extraordinary connections. The things he
finds. Look at these chocolate biscuits.

She has pulled him to the table. Peter notices Ann at a
distance.

Vi She wouldn't let any of us touch them.

Betty Take off your coat.

Peter stares at Ann.

Peter (*smiles*) I didn't know. [About the pregnancy].

Ann One more surprise.

Peter (*to Mike*) Congratulations.

Mike I mentioned on the way here about work in the
surgery. We could use another pair of –.

Ann Later, Mike. Later. He's just got here.

Peter tries to stop Betty fussing.

Peter Betty . . .

He touches her hand, looks her in the eyes. She suddenly turns away and begins to cry. For a moment no one knows what to do. Ann goes and holds her.

Mike It's a small surgery. Just me and another doctor. You'd get to do a number of things. Check in patients. We need the help. It's not charity.

Ann Mike . . .

Peter Thank you.

Betty continues to sob on Ann's shoulder.

Mike Betty is our nurse.

Peter I know.

Vi Sit down, please, Peter.

Ann How was the journey?

Peter I missed a connection in Toronto. But I caught up. I met two – 'boys' my age, who I hadn't seen since the trip over. Strange.

Mike You were in –.

Vi (*answering for him*) Alberta. (*Beat.*) That's the left-hand side part. (*looking at Peter*) You look like Father.

She turns to Betty, who is trying to calm down and who nods in agreement, staring at Peter.

Peter (*still standing with suitcase*) Should I put –??

Betty (*breathing deeply, wiping away her tears*) Mike and Ann, of course, have Mother and Father's room. Vi's moved in with me. So you have your old room back.

Peter I didn't need my old –.

3

Vi Father's library and the bathroom we had to give up.

Peter (*confused*) When –? (*to Betty*) You never wrote –.

Vi (*explaining*) They're another flat now.

Betty What was there to write?

Vi Maybe in a while –. Mike thinks – we might get them back. Put it all back together. We have the kitchen.

Betty (*still staring*) I used to bathe you. (*She smiles.*) Please sit down. (*to the others*) He's a man.

After a beat, this makes the others laugh.

Vi What did you expect?!

The laughter dies down. Awkward pause – what to say after so many years.

Mike (*finally*) I'm looking forward to hearing about Canada. It's a place . . .

Peter That you'd like to visit?

Mike Not particularly. (*He smiles.*)

Peter (*to Ann and Vi*) And I'm interested in hearing all about Wales.

Ann What's to tell? (*She shrugs.*)

Peter And Vi, you're acting.

Betty (*to Ann*) Listen to his accent.

Ann I know.

Peter has an American/Canadian accent.

Betty (*answering Peter*) Did you ever think she'd do anything else?

Peter Mother would be pleased.

4

Betty I don't think so.

Peter Father?

They react, shake heads, laugh – of course he wouldn't be pleased.

Vi I had an audition this morning. Do you know *Autumn Fire*?

Ann (*over this*) It was on at the Duchess –.

Betty (*over this*) We saw it –. When did we see it?

Peter I don't know anything! I've been in Canada!

Laughter.

Betty It's very good.

Vi The part's Peggy. She's –.

Betty (*over this*) Tell him who Peggy is.

Vi She –.

Ann (*before she can explain*) Just do the bit. What you did for the audition.

Vi But he just got here.

Peter No, I don't [mind] –

Mike Which one is Peggy?

Betty Sh-sh.

Ann Show him.

Vi walks out, then returns as 'Peggy'.

Vi/Peggy 'Hen, dear. It's been ages.' (*Pretends to kiss 'Hen'.*) 'And Howard darling. You don't look ill at all. Or aren't you? (*trying to figure it out*) Or wasn't that you? Is that brandy we're drinking? (*Takes a sip of 'Howard's*

5

*glass'.) Mmmmm. Thank you, I was nearly sober. And –
who – is – that?' (Points to an imaginary man.)* Hen says:
'Have you met my cousin, Peter?'

Betty *(making a connection where there isn't any, to Peter)*
The character's name is Peter.

Vi/Peggy 'And where, Hen, have you been hiding such a
man? Under your bed?' *(She holds out her hand for the
imaginary man to shake.)* 'You – I'll see later.' *(As she
walks across the room, to the imaginary Hen)* 'A family
secret, I suppose. Or is it – treasure.'

Mike I'm going to pour myself a drink. *(to Peter)* Anyone –?

Betty He's only –.

Vi/Peggy sinks into a chair.

Vi/Peggy 'There wasn't a living thing in all of Paris. Only
the French.'

Betty *(to Mike)* He doesn't want a drink.

*Peter notices the photographs on the small table, though
he continues to watch Vi's audition.*
   *Vi/Peggy sits, smoothing her crossed legs with her
hand, as she continues:*

Vi/Peggy 'What a simply horrid week abroad. Thank God
for champagne, or I'd actually remember it.'

*Mike laughs, then Betty does, looking at Mike. Ann
watches Peter who has picked up a framed photo, but is
still watching.*

'What possessed me? No, I shall never again stray. I make
this my oath, upon pain of death, never again shall I ven-
ture forth off this great island of civility, of kindness and
beauty, and into the filthy God-forsaken seas which sur-
round it.'

Ann (*to Peter*) Then one of the characters –.

Betty (*explaining over this*) Howard.

Ann (*continuing*) – asks, 'So you'll never leave England again?'

Vi/Peggy 'England?! Who said anything about England? I was talking about – the Savoy.'

Laughter, and the audition is over. Peter sets the photo back down and applauds.

Ann (*teasing*) Maybe Mother wouldn't be happy.

Laughter.

Vi (*all shyness*) Peggy's supposed to be in her thirties. I told them I thought I was too young.

Betty You should let them decide –.

Vi The tour's Grimsby, Warrington, Liskeard, and some-where else, I forget. (*Beat.*) They'll let me know. Maybe this week. (*She suddenly feels terribly awkward, everyone looking at her. Embarrassed*) Why did I do that? Of all things to –. He just got . . .

She turns away, quickly turns back to see Peter smiling and looking at her.

What? Why are you staring?

He suddenly goes and hugs her. This makes Betty start to cry again.

Peter Betty, please . . .

Betty Listen to that accent!

Peter I'm sorry, but . . .

Betty I didn't say that it was bad.

Vi breaks away, and being very much the child now:

Vi As long as Mother and Father don't find out.

She hurries to the photo Peter was looking at and turns it face down. Again laughter. Mike hands Peter a drink.

Mike Here.

Betty He's seventeen years old!

Mike (*sipping his drink*) My point exactly.

Peter What I'd love is a cup of tea.

Vi I'll put the kettle on –.

Betty (*at the same time*) I'll get it –. (*Turns to Vi.*) You do the kettle. I'll take his bag into his room. And see if the bed's made.

Vi I made it.

Betty And see if the bed's made – correctly.

Betty and Vi hurry off, leaving Peter with Ann and Mike. After another short, awkward pause.

Mike I'm standing there outside the buffet, holding up this photo – he goes by me – what two or three times? (*He laughs and ruffles Peter's hair as if he were a boy.*)

Ann As long as it worked out – in the end. That's all that counts. (*She looks at Peter, then:*) Come here.

Vi (*off, she shouts*) I'm so happy!!

Ann (*to Peter*) Come here.

Peter goes to her and she holds him, strokes his hair.

I don't know what to say.

She turns back to Mike who now sits, smiling, sipping his drink.

8

She turns back to Peter, begins to kiss his cheeks, rub his hair, hug him, repeating:

Look at you. Look at you. Look at you.

SCENE TWO

The same later that evening.
   Peter sits, plate of food in his lap. The others have eaten, plates to their side or on the floor, or they have chosen not to eat.

Ann At first – they seemed really nice. I was treated like I was someone special.

Peter It was the same with me. Then –.

Vi I didn't have this problem.

Ann That's not true.

Vi She talks about this and –.

Ann You got as upset as I did.

Peter (*to Betty*) You started to feel like they were thinking is this kid ever going home?

Ann (*to Vi*) I saw how they looked at you. And how they looked at me. (*to Peter*) They adored the little ones.

Peter In Wales you had to work?

Vi Work! What else did we do? What else did I do. I practically took care of her.

Ann That's completely untrue! I was like – the mother, for God's sake.

Vi I don't believe this.

Ann From the moment at the station, standing there with

9

our little luggage labels with our names on them around our necks. When Mother let go of my hand – she put it in yours. I knew what she was saying. I was fourteen years old! But I held on. When they tried to separate us – who screamed? (*Beat.*) Who took her fist and began hitting the lady who was trying to push my sister away into another queue? We're a family, I said. You can't separate us. (*Beat.*) We're all we have. (*Beat.*) This big house – the school was in one side, we slept in the other. This was for about a month. Then we billeted with a couple. We slept together. (*Beat.*) Vi and me. (*Beat.*) He was a miner. He'd have his bath – we'd get our 'Uncle's' bath ready – by the fire, then – off we go. Get out. Into the winter, summer – outside. Off you go. And wait. Sometimes we went to the pictures. Until Mum and Dad . . . And we weren't being sent any more money.

Betty I sent you money.

Ann That's true.

Pause.

Vi They had a dog. A really nice dog – at the school. We loved the dog. A bit of a labrador. Black. He began to follow me around. (*to Ann*) Remember? (*back to Peter*) I took care of him. He slept at the foot of our bed. (*Beat.*) I went to school. Came back. He was gone. He'd been volunteered to the army. Sniffing land mines in Belgium. I cried more than when Mum and Dad died.

Short pause.

Peter Just a couple of days after I got to my 'Aunt' and 'Uncle's' – their big black and white cat had kittens. Nine. I was so – happy. To see them. Some – things – that – knew, understood – even less than me. (*smiles, takes a bite.*)

Vi (*to Betty*) I know what he [means] –.

Peter So my 'Auntie', I suppose, seeing my – pleasure? She says, choose one, Petey.

Ann Petey?

His sisters giggle.

Peter It happened. I don't know how –.

Betty Petey!!!

Peter (*over their giggling*) Choose one! We'll have to drown the rest.

The girls stop giggling.

I look at those kittens in the barn. Each one. I touch each – one. And I couldn't choose. It wasn't right to choose, I felt. Auntie got impatient with me, and she drowned them all. (*Pause.*) When they put me in the field to work? I was put with some Negroes. I said to 'Uncle' – I'm a white man, I'm not a Negro. And he took the palm of his hand and rammed it into my head. I think I was passed out for about ten minutes. (*Beat.*) For weeks I thought about why he did that.

Betty He was probably trying to tell you that Negroes were just as good as white people. He thought you were –.

Peter I thought of that. Sometimes I thought that was the reason.

Beat.

Vi Maybe he just didn't like someone questioning him.

Peter Maybe. (*Shrugs.*) In school there a kid hit me because he said I had an uppity accent.

Betty You don't have a –.

11

Peter Then. I lost it. So maybe Uncle heard . . . (*Shrugs again.*) I never knew. (*Beat.*) I feel there's so much I don't know.

Ann (*agreeing with his confusion*) Were we supposed to work or not? Were we sent – to work? Was that part of the plan?

Vi We were sent to be safe –?

Ann Why did I have to work? Margaret Wells? She came with us. We were on the same train. We were at the same school –. She didn't work. Her 'Auntie' taught her things. She had, I think, two beautiful dresses that her 'Auntie' embroidered . . . (*Beat.*) I've often wondered – did they put us together for reasons? How did they – match us? Did they know something about us – me? Or was it all –? When we got off the train –. No one had bothered to tell me this. (*to Vi*) You didn't tell me this –.

Vi (*over this*) What??

Ann I'd obviously touched some soot on the train, and touched my face with my hand – I saw it later in a window – there was a streak of soot across my head. (*Shakes her head and smiles.*) Maybe when we were standing in the queue? Being – picked? If I hadn't had that soot on my face – would I have learned to embroider like Margaret Wells? Would I have been picked earlier, by someone – else? (*Short pause. To Peter*) You're not eating.

He holds up his plate, she takes it, looks at him, strokes his hair.

Peter I should go and unpack. (*He doesn't move.*)

Betty (*to Mike*) This must be boring for you.

Mike No, no. It's not. I'll get another drink. (*He gets up and goes to get a drink, stops.*) But just don't start blaming all those people. They interrupted their lives for all of you. They were heroes, in my mind. (*He goes off into the kitchen.*)

Betty (*to Peter*) He's a nice man. A good doctor.

Vi He pays for all [this] –

Betty I work.

Vi He and Betty.

Betty He's been very good to us all. Hasn't he, Ann?

No response. This catches Peter's interest.

(*to Peter*) She's never satisfied.

Ann (*suddenly upset*) How dare you say that?!

Betty If I can't say it, then who –

Ann (*over this*) Shut up! I said, shut up, Betty.

Peter (*over this to Vi*) What's??

Vi ignores the question. Just as suddenly as they erupted, there is silence.

(*to Ann*) How did you and Mike – meet?

Vi He works with Betty.

Betty (*correcting*) I work with him.

Vi Betty brought him home.

Betty To meet my sisters. I had a crush on him myself, then.

She laughs, no one else does.

Ann and he make a wonderful couple. You knew that right away. They'll have a wonderful baby.

Ann He's a nice man. As she says.

Betty Mother would have liked him. She would have approved. She was trying to become a nurse, you know.

Peter I didn't –.

Betty First it was a schoolteacher, then after the three of you went away, it was a nurse. She hadn't got that far when . . . It's why she was out that day. (*Beat.*) Mike, it turns out – isn't the world strange? It turns out was there as well. So she could have been one of the people he helped pull out. He helped pull people out from under all the . . . (*Beat.*) I have often wondered . . .

Vi Father is buried in France. You knew that?

Peter nods.

Betty They sent us a ring. We don't think it was Father's ring.

Mike returns with a drink. For a moment no one says anything. As he passes, Mike strokes Ann's head; she doesn't respond.

Vi (*finally*) At school they had attached a bell to a tree. We were told that if we spotted any enemy parachutists to run and ring that bell. (*Beat.*) I could see the tree from my seat in the classroom. I used to daydream that like large snowflakes suddenly the sky was filled with parachutes. And no one else saw them. Everyone else was too busy – learning things. I ran out of the classroom. Reached the tree and the bell and began ringing it with all my strength. Soldiers suddenly arrived and captured all the bad people. Dad was always one of the soldiers. (*Pause.*)

Peter *I* used to dream of you. [All of them.] (*He stands and goes and hugs each one in turn.*) I should unpack.

He starts to go, but is stopped by:

Ann Vi was in a nativity play – playing Joseph.

14

Peter Joseph??

Vi 'Uncle' drew with coal on my face to make the whiskers.

Ann She didn't know who Joseph was.

Vi (*same time*) I didn't know who Joseph –.

Ann Then she's told he's – Mary's husband. And I tell her like Dad is Mum's husband. So she's there in the nativity, and everyone is watching, and she says: 'Mary, give me a drink.'

> *Peter and his sisters all say: 'Just like Father!!' and laugh.*
> *Still smiling, Peter goes down the hallway to his bedroom. The others stop laughing.*
> *The sisters start to pick up the plates, etc.*

Betty He's got – so old.

Mike He's a boy.

Vi (*ignoring Mike*) I thought I'd faint when I saw him.

Ann He looks like Father.

Vi I see Mother.

Betty He used to be –. He'd never sit still.

Ann (*over this*) He's tired. Think about what we look like to him.

Vi And the flat.

Ann It must be . . .

Vi (*to Mike*) God it must be a relief for you – to finally have another man around! (*She smiles.*)

Mike He's a boy.

Vi (*over this*) Some – reinforcements against all us women!

Mike I haven't minded. In fact, I've rather enjoyed it.

He laughs, as do Betty and Vi. As Vi picks up a plate, he leans over and tries to 'pinch' her and she 'squeals' – all a game they've played before. Vi starts to head for the kitchen, laughing. As she goes, we hear Peter calling her, 'Vi!' She turns and hurries down the hallway to Peter. Ann shows no reaction to the pinching.

Betty (*to Mike*) So what do you think?

Mike He's a fine boy. I like him.

Betty I knew you would.

Mike And I think we should be able to find a place for him in the surgery.

Ann And not just sweeping floors, he needs to learn –.

Mike I'll supervise his duties myself.

Betty Thank you.

Beat.

Ann I mean it, Mike. Don't make promises you can't keep.

This stops the room for a moment, then Betty turns to Mike.

Betty You've been so good to us.

Mike (*shrugs*) Remember I had a son. Not much older than your Pete.

Betty (*suddenly smiling*) Or Petey as we now must call him!

She laughs.
    Suddenly Peter comes out of the hall wearing a full cowboy costume – chaps, hat, vest, spurs.

Peter (*bursting in*) Howdy, English folk!

Laughter.

And this is how they really dress in Alberta! (*He carries a couple of packages under his arm.*)

Ann I don't believe –.

Peter Except on Sunday for church, then they wear their fancy clothes! Hat's out to [here] –.

But he is interrupted by Vi who appears in Indian clothes (her present from Peter). She has taken off her dress and put on a little Indian vest over her slip, hoisted up the slip and put on the skirt – looking sexy and a bit indecent. The others react, laughing.

Peter And here is Viohantas, Indian Squaw!! (*Turns to Betty.*) And this is for you, Betty. (*to Ann*) And for you. (*Hands out their presents. To Mike*) I'm sorry, but I didn't gct –.

Mike Please.

Peter And I didn't know about the baby when –.

Betty (*opening her package*) Where did you get the money? (*She opens the box, takes out a blouse. She immediately turns away, takes off her blouse and puts on the new one.*)

Mike (*during this*) I'm turning away.

The new blouse is low cut, exposing her bra.

Betty How's this?

Peter (*goes and touches her bra strap*) You can't wear that with it.

Betty (*stunned, to her sisters*) Since when did our brother become a woman's fashion expert –? (*But she turns, glances at Mike.*)

Mike I'm not looking!

She turns, takes off the blouse, then her bra, then starts to put the blouse back on. As she does, Ann opens her present – jewellery.

Ann It's gorgeous, Peter! Where did you –?

Peter It didn't cost much.

Vi, getting into being an Indian:

Vi Remember we used to ride on Betty? She used to give Pete and –.

Ann Petey!

Vi (*grabbing Betty*) Come on! Around the room!

Betty (*adjusting her blouse, ignoring Vi*) What do you think? I don't think I could wear this out –.

Vi Get down.

Betty gets down, but continues to 'ignore' Vi.

Peter (*to Betty*) Perhaps it's not meant to wear out, but rather – at home. With – whomever?

He smiles. She nods, smiles, catches a quick look at Mike, then turns away.

Betty I'll wear it around the house then.

Vi Come on, horsey. Let's go. Come on!

Vi is on the back of Betty who is down on all fours, though still seemingly oblivious to Vi.

Ann (*at the same time, holding the necklace*) Peter, help me put it on.

He goes to help. Vi now rides Betty, who constantly fiddles with the new blouse as her breasts are nearly uncovered (though no one seems to notice).

Vi (*on Betty*) Faster! Let's attack those Germans!

Peter I think she's mixing up her wars.

Vi Yahoo!!!

Ann (*to Peter*) I love it. (*Kisses him on the cheek.*)

Vi Petey! You're next! Come on! Give her a ride! Come on!

Betty (*to Mike*) He used to do this all the time –.

Ann Come on!

She drags him to Betty. Vi gets off, Peter gets on reluctantly, though doesn't put his whole weight on her. Betty rides around, begins to buck (as she used to when he was a small child). Others laugh as he tries to hold on – then the phone rings. This calms everyone down. Mike takes the call, then:

Mike (*to Vi*) It's for you.

Vi takes it. Betty 'whinnies' quietly, Peter slaps her bottom as he would a horse.

Betty Oh really!

She suddenly bucks and he nearly falls off. Vi hangs up:

Vi I didn't get the part. The director.

Beat.

Betty I'm sorry . . .

Ann I thought you wouldn't hear until –.

Vi He says he thinks I'm talented though. He wants to have lunch.

Ann He's after you?

Vi doesn't respond, then:

Vi And he's something like twenty years older than me. (*Then she realizes what she has just said in Mike's presence.*)

Mike God, then he must have a foot in death's door.

He smiles, others laugh. The faux pas is forgotten, or forgiven.

Ann (*suddenly to Vi*) Do you remember that when we used to play hide and seek, on rainy days, there was always a place that Peter would hide – and we never found him.

Betty I remember that.

Vi I don't remember.

Ann Maybe you were too young. Maybe she didn't play.

Vi I'm older than Peter.

Ann He was a boy.

Vi What's that –?

Ann Where was that place, Peter?

They look at him, then:

Peter Start counting.

Ann What –?

Betty (*over this*) What are we –?

Peter Count!

Ann looks at the others, then covers her face and begins to count. Peter and Betty start to go off and hide. Betty hesitates, then goes in a different direction. Peter goes off towards the kitchen.

Mike (*to Vi*) Hide!

Vi (*whispers*) Where?!

Mike (*whispers*) Anywhere?

He suggests behind the sofa. She hurries there, just as Ann finishes her count.

Ann Coming, ready or not –.

Peter walks back in. The others look at him.

Peter It was behind the ironing board in the kitchen cupboard. There's a hole. It's still there. (*Beat.*) But now I don't fit.

SCENE THREE

The same. The next morning.
Peter, barefoot, sits, his legs over the arm of a chair, a book in his lap. (He had been reading and is interrupted by Vi.) Vi stands in front of a mirror, straightening her clothes, fixing her hair. She wears her best clothes. As she fixes she talks:

Vi First this girl says to her 'family' that she can't take communion. Her 'Auntie' is all upset – we have a heathen in the house! We've taken in a heathen! Then she has to tell them, well – it's because I'm a Catholic.

Betty enters, dressed. She carries toast on a plate.

So she can't take communion.

Betty (*who has heard the story*) But then she does.

Vi That's right.

Betty (*beginning to eat the toast*) And she writes to her mother and obviously –.

21

Vi You weren't even there. (*Turns back to Peter.*) Writes to her mother and her mother writes to the local Catholic priest and he comes to the house. And the girl tells him that, yes, she's taken communion in the Protestant church and –.

Betty And she rather liked it.

Vi And so the priest, he says to her, child you will never again be allowed to take communion in a Roman Catholic service. (*Beat.*) Ten years old and he excommunicated her.

She leans over and begins to draw a line down the back of her leg – to look like a stocking seam.

Finally they had to find another family for her. She became – nervous. (*She finishes the seam, and turns to Betty to explain her clothes.*) They're making a picture in Leicester Square. (*Reaches for the newspaper, tosses it to Betty.*) Looking for people to be society. You have to bring your own clothes. Pays a guinea for the day. And lunch. (*Turns back to Peter.*) How did we get started talking about . . .?

Suddenly, with newspaper still in hand, Betty goes to Vi and tries to lift up her skirt.

(*to Betty, pushing her hand away*) What are you –? Stop it!

Peter Betty?!!

Vi Get away from me!

Beat.

Betty (*explaining*) I just wanted to –. To make sure she was wearing her drawers.

Vi Why wouldn't I –??

Betty (*to Peter*) Her audition yesterday? She came home and told me – while you were waiting to go in, she was sitting next to a girl. Vi notices her lift up her skirt – to cross her legs – and nothing. (*She turns to Vi.*) So –? What?

Vi says nothing. Betty continues to explain.

So what does she say to Vi? You're staring at her and what does this 'actress' say?!

Vi (*quietly*) 'We'll see who gets the part.'

Peter That's disgusting.

Betty Isn't it.

Vi That's not what it's usually like. And you don't have to tell everyone –.

Betty He's your brother! And he's a man. What do you think about that – as a man?

Peter I said, I thought it was disgusting.

Betty He's disgusted, Vi.

Vi She didn't get the part!

Betty How do you know that? Did you get it?! (*She reaches to look again under Vi's skirt.*)

Vi It's not even an audition. It's only an extra!!!

Betty flips up the skirt. Vi has her drawers on. Betty lets the skirt fall. Vi is upset, nearly in tears. She moves away from her sister.

I have to go. Excuse me. Where's my hat?

Peter gestures.

Betty Let me get the shopping money and I'll walk with you as far as the tube.

She goes to the kitchen. Peter and Vi look at each other for a moment.

Peter (*to say something*) Betty doesn't have to work today?

Vi The surgery doesn't open until noon on Tuesdays.

Peter But Mike left –.

Vi He goes to the hospital on Tuesday mornings. (*Beat.*) Betty does the shopping on Tuesdays. Ann used to do it but with . . .

Betty has returned with coat and bag.

Betty (*more explanation*) And I don't mind one bit either. Ann shouldn't be carrying heavy . . . anything. Mike wouldn't hear of it, for one. (*to Vi*) He's so – thoughtful. Mike. Isn't he?

Vi nods.

We think Ann's the luckiest woman in the world. Don't we?

Vi hesitates, then nods. Short pause. Betty stands looking at Peter.

Peter What?

Beat.

Betty Seeing you there, like that – with a book. You know what I just remembered? What I just realized I miss? Sitting around – together – all reading together. To each other.

Vi When have we ever done that?

Betty (*staring at Peter*) Not for years.

Beat.

24

Vi Did Mother used to read to us?

Peter (*shakes his head*) No, Father did. (*to Betty*) For what? About a month? He'd come home from the newspaper and he'd read to us. Religiously – for a month. Then it just stopped. (*He shrugs.*) Why?

Betty I don't know.

Vi How do you remember and I don't?

Peter (*over this*) It's a good thought. We should do it.

Betty Now that we're all together.

Peter Exactly.

    Beat.

Betty I feel like I don't know anything.

Peter (*holding up his book*) I doubt if Zane Grey is going to make you feel –.

Betty It's a start.

    She turns, notices something about Vi's collar that isn't right, so she straightens it as a mother might. Then without saying anything more, they leave.
    Peter puts down his book, goes to the screen or clothes rack and tub that lean against a wall. Sets the tub upright, places the screen/rack around the tub, then heads off to the kitchen.
    After a moment, Ann enters from her bedroom. She wears a dressing gown. She goes and sits on the sofa, stands, turns on the radio, quickly turns it off. Sees the leftover piece of toast, takes a bite.
    Peter returns carrying two large buckets of water for his bath.

Ann God, are my sisters loud.

Peter Did we wake you?

Ann You didn't.

Peter I'm going to take a bath. Is that all –?

Ann You live here, Peter.

He smiles, nods, goes behind the screen and begins to pour the water in.
    Ann watches, then:

We had such a nice bath, remember? It had little feet and little claws. So you could pretend you were on some animal. Or flying bird.

Peter pours the second bucket.

Peter I never pretended that. (*Beat.*) But it was a nice big tub.

Short pause.

Ann But now we have a telephone. (*She looks at the phone.*) That's something good. Better. (*explaining*) Because of Mike and the surgery –.

Peter I assumed.

Ann So we mustn't assume that everything just gets worse.

Peter looks at her. She looks away, rubs herself.

I think I pee twenty times a night. Did *I* wake *you*?

Peter (*as he heads back to the kitchen with the buckets*) I slept like a baby.

Ann You're home.

Peter's gone.

Peter (*off*) What?!

Ann (*calling*) I said you're –.

*She stops herself. Takes another bite of toast. Looks at
Peter's book.*
  He returns with another bucket.

I said you're home.

  He looks at her. He's forgotten the conversation.

Never mind. Where's . . .?

Peter Vi's gone to be in a picture. Betty's shopping. (*He
goes to pour the water into the tub.*)

Ann I used to go shopping.

Peter But now you have to be careful what you carry.

Ann Do I? Is that warm?

Peter I've been heating it on the stove. (*He goes again.*)

Ann (*continuing the shopping drift*) The queues are for-
ever! You need the patience of Job!

  *Peter's gone, Ann continues but really to herself or no
  one.*

Or nothing else to do. And that is just the impression you
get standing in some of those endless queues – that people
now have nothing to do. (*Beat.*) Or nothing they want to
do.

  Peter returns with another bucket.

Peter So now Betty does the shopping. That must be
great for you. (*He starts to go to the tub.*)

Ann (*holding up his book*) You reading this?

Peter Yes, I –.

Ann (*reading the inscription*) 'To Petey from your Auntie
Fay.'

Peter She gave it to me as a going away –.

Ann *Riders of the Purple Sage*. Kids' book?

Peter Not necessarily.

Ann Looks like a kids' book.

Peter It's –.

Ann Do you miss her?

> *Beat.*

Peter What??

Ann Do you miss her? 'Auntie Fay'? (*more adamant*) Do you miss being called Petey?!! When you left we called you Peter!!

> *Short pause. Peter goes behind the screen and pours the water into the tub. He comes out – sets down the bucket.*

Full?

Peter Enough.

Ann What do you remember of Mother?

> *Peter is stopped by this.*

Betty remembers – so much more than me. But then she was here. She wasn't sent away. She was the lucky one – right?

Peter (*after a beat*) Yes.

Ann Is that what you think?

Peter Ann –.

Ann (*almost yelling*) That she was the lucky one?! I'll tell you about your sister. Put this in your head. (*Beat.*) When Mother took Vi and me to the station, Betty was with us of course. She's told me, walking home with Mother, Mother all of a sudden fell on to the pavement and started sobbing. She hit her fists against a wall. She crawled. Betty, who wasn't very large – isn't, but certainly wasn't then – tried to pick her up. (*Beat.*) At sixteen she suddenly saw a lot. When Mother died, Father was home on leave. So when the telegram came, Betty had to read it – to Father, who because it was ever so slightly ambiguously written kept saying – but there's still hope, isn't there? Isn't there? Please tell me that there is hope. (*Beat.*) So she had to convince him. Convince those two sky-blue watery eyes. Convince Father that Mother was – gone. (*Beat.*) Lucky her.

Peter I didn't –.

Ann Take your bath.

Peter just looks at her.

(*to herself, rubbing her eyes*) I need sleep. (*She reaches over and turns the radio back on – dance music plays.*) Young man, there are things you don't know . . . (*She shrugs.*) Come here.

Peter comes to her.

Raise your arms.

Peter What? Why –?

Ann I said, raise your arms.

Peter is confused, but he raises his arms. She looks at him seriously, then suddenly tickles him hard in the armpits. He pulls away.

(*laughing*) You are such a sucker! You always were! Do you do everything anyone asks you to do?!

Peter looks at her totally confused.

Grow up. Take your bath. It's getting cold.

Peter turns and heads for the screen.

Not only does he sound like a Canadian. He's come back with the wits of one!

Peter stops, thinks of what to say, says nothing, then goes behind the screen to take his clothes off and get into the bath.

Do you mind if I stay . . .?

No response. She listens to the radio for a moment. Behind the screen Peter is undressed. We hear him get into the water.

Did Betty tell you we're having company tonight?

Peter (*off, behind the screen*) Some doctor –.

Ann I tried to tell Mike – your first full day here, why do we need –.

Peter (*off*) He's trying to help me, Ann.

Beat.

Ann Hugh. That's the man's name. Hugh. (*Beat.*) Betty's been trying to hook him.

Peter (*off*) That's not the impression –.

Ann (*over this*) And God knows I hope she does. Maybe then she'd move those doe-eyes of hers off my husband.

Peter (*off*) Ann, I don't want to –.

Ann (*over this*) Not that he doesn't encourage her. Not that he doesn't encourage all of them. Wait till you see his other nurse – she looks like she's twelve. He likes them young, that should be clear. (*Beat.*) Isn't it?

No response.

Peter?

30

Peter (*off, behind the screen*) This doctor, Betty said, was invited so I could meet him. Mike's trying to give me a choice. This man needs help too.

   Beat.

Ann Oh. So that's the reason he's invited. I'm sorry – I got it all terribly wrong.

Peter (*off*) Ann, Betty said –.

Ann Oh, Betty said. Betty said! Let me tell you something – you believe everything your sisters tell you, Petey, and I fear for your future.

   Beat. Then Peter suddenly finds this funny and laughs. Ann smiles and laughs too.

Peter (*off*) I don't care why this Hugh is –.

Ann Sh-shh! I like this.

   A song has come on the radio she likes. It is 'Goodnight Children Everywhere'. Peter listens as well, so that for a moment we don't hear the water moving around.

Radio
   Goodnight children, everywhere
   Your mummy thinks of you tonight.
   Lay your head upon your pillow,
   Don't be a kid or a weeping willow.
   Close your eyes and say a prayer
   And surely you can find a kiss to spare.
   Though you are far away
   She's with you night and day.
   Goodnight children, everywhere.

Ann (*over this*) Vi and I had a special signal when this came on. We'd snap our fingers . . . (*She snaps them.*) . . . and it meant 'Mother'. That I was thinking about Mother. And . . . (*two snaps*) Father. No one else knew.

Radio (*song continues*)
 Sleepy little eyes and sleepy little head
 Sleepy time is drawing near
 In a little while
 You'll be tucked up in your bed
 Here's a song for baby dear:
 Goodnight children, everywhere . . .

 *The pain is nearly unbearable, finally Ann turns it off
 before it finishes.*

Peter (*off*) They played that in Alberta too. Some
American lady sang it.

 *Pause. Then from behind the screen Peter snaps his fin-
 gers once. Ann nearly collapses when she hears. She
 then snaps once as well.*

(*off*) When the letter arrived about – Mother, Auntie read
it to me. They'd sent it to her, to open it. (*We hear him
play with the water, slap it – to do something.*) Auntie
read it out loud over the kitchen table, then folded the letter very carefully, put it back into the envelope, then
handed it all to me. (*Beat.*) She kissed my head and said,
they are savages. In Europe, that's what they are. No better. And then she took me outside – into their garden –
and pointed to the mountains. There, Auntie said, is a
better world. Mountains don't lie. Mountains don't cheat.
They don't murder. They don't make war. And then we
both cried.

 *Ann picks up the photo on the table and looks at her
 parents.*

That night, she brought out photos of Mother.

 *Ann is amazed by the coincidence of picking up a photo
 and having Peter, who can't see her, mention photos.*

Not at all like those on the table there. Of Mother and

Auntie dancing. (*Beat.*) You knew that Mother had been a dancer –.

Ann I think maybe I forgot.

Peter (*off*) Really? So maybe that's where Vi gets her acting –.

Ann I don't know.

 Beat.

Peter (*off*) In fur coats. With their arms around each other. Kicking out a leg. Auntie had spent two years in London. They looked like children. Mother and her. Younger even – than us. With big smiles on their faces. Auntie said they were best friends. For those two years. (*Beat.*) It's how Mother met Father – dancing.

Ann What??

Peter (*off*) According to Auntie. And she was there. (*Beat.*) There was another photo – they're in some costume with feathers, black shoes with a strap across –.

Ann Maryjanes.

Peter (*off*) I kept asking Auntie – what's this? When was this? She said, she couldn't remember. She just had the photos. (*Beat.*) Then she pulled out one of us. Betty, Vi, you and me. I couldn't be more than two. (*Beat.*) There we were sitting in a drawer, thousands of miles away from here. (*Beat.*) I didn't even know Mother knew her. I thought she was a farmer's wife. Then she brought out the photos.

 Short pause.

Ann I had to look through Mother's clothes. There was a dress – like that. With feathers. I thought it was . . . for a party. It's still in the cupboard . . .

33

She goes to talk to Peter behind the screen, we hear him splash as he tries to cover himself up.

Peter (*off*) Ann! (*Short pause.*) What are you staring at?

Ann Nothing. Nothing. (*She comes back out.*) I'll get that dress out. Wouldn't it be great if it is the one in the photograph you saw? (*She goes and looks in the mirror.*) I could try it on . . . (*Short pause.*) Mike thinks I'm going to stay fat.

Peter (*off*) You're not fat, you're pregnant! Did he say –?

Ann It's what he thinks. His first wife was terribly skinny.

Peter (*off*) I didn't know he had a first –.

Ann She was young too. Then she got older. Why did you give Betty and Vi those pretty clothes and me a necklace?

Peter (*off*) What?

Ann goes again behind the screen.

Ann (*off*) Why did you do that, Peter?

Peter (*off*) Ann!!!

Short pause.

Ann (*off, quietly*) What's that?

He has an erection.

Peter (*off*) I'm sorry.

Ann (*off*) Don't be. Me?

Peter (*off*) Ann, I'm trying to take a –.

Ann (*still from behind the screen*) The first erection I ever saw, he was a miner, he was all black.

Peter (*off*) I don't want to know, Ann.

Pause.

Ann (*off*) You going to do something with that?

Peter (*off*) It'll – calm down.

Ann (*off*) Will it?

Peter (*off*) Not if you keep staring at it.

Ann (*off*) And if I touch it?

Peter (*off*) Ann, what are you . . .?

From behind the screen, we hear the water move around as Ann touches Peter.

Ann (*off*) If you don't want me to . . . Say something.

Peter (*off*) Ann.

Ann (*off*) Something besides Ann.

She is masturbating him. The water sounds get quicker, as her hand moves quicker, then splashing, then he comes.
      Silence.
      Ann comes out from behind the screen, trying to dry the arm she has just had in the water. She is shaking.
      She sits, unable to say anything. From behind the screen no sound whatsoever.

(*finally*) Mind if I turn on the radio?

She does. Music. We hear Peter get out of the bath. He puts on his trousers and comes out, holding his shirt. As he reaches Ann, she grabs his shirt.

Look at that. Let me darn it.

He stands uncomfortably, not knowing what to do with himself, with his hands, etc. Music continues on the radio.

(*with the shirt*) My God was there no one looking after you? (*She gets the sewing box and sits. After a moment she looks up, smiles at him, then begins to darn. As she sews*) At school in Wales, there was this big sign – official poster from the government. 'What girls can do to win the war.' What jobs –. Like –. (*Nods to her darning.*) 'Study your sewing machine,' it said. 'Snug slippers from old felt hats.' But we didn't have any old felt hats in Wales. Things to fix – so you wouldn't depend upon – I suppose your father. Get used to him not . . . there?? 'When a drawer sticks.' Vi and I used to pretend that our 'drawers' were stuck –

Mimes underpants stuck. She looks at Peter who smiles.

They can get a child to believe anything.

Peter comes up to her. He is still shirtless, sockless. He looks at her from behind, holds her shoulders. She sighs and leans back.

I'm sorry.

He touches her hair, then leans down and tries to kiss her.

No!!

She pushes him back and slaps his hand. He is very confused now.

No. (*She rubs her eyes, then:*) Some days I lie awake in bed and I think – but I'm still a child myself. What the hell am I doing having a baby? (*Beat.*) But I'll be a good mother. Won't I?

He hesitates, then nods.

I think I'm ready. I was like a mother to Vi for so long. (*Beat.*) And before that, before you – left – to you.

Peter I thought Betty mostly –.

Ann We shared. She dressed you. (*Beat.*) I bathed you.

Suddenly the door bursts open and Vi enters. Ann and Peter nearly jump, and move quickly and guiltily away from each other.

Vi (*as she enters, noticing nothing*) It's raining! They won't be shooting outside. At least I didn't waste my money on the tube. (*She is off, down the hall to her room.*)

Ann (*to Peter*) Have you finished your bath?

Beat. Peter goes and turns the tub over into a drain. As the water pours out, Vi returns, having taken off her blouse. She carries another shirt. She wears a bra but doesn't seem in the least bit self-conscious in front of her brother.

Vi So what are you two doing today?

Ann I have some cleaning and washing –.

Vi Peter, what about you?

Ann (*over this*) Mike's asked him to drop by the surgery this afternoon. See what he thinks.

Peter I don't think I'm ready for that yet. I think I want to take my time before –.

Vi Then come to the pictures with me!! (*She puts her arm in his, still both shirtless.*) I hate going alone. A girl alone – they come out of the woodwork. (*to Ann*) Don't they?

Ann I wouldn't –.

Vi (*to Peter*) Come on, protect me! I'll put my arm around you and pretend you're my big boyfriend. (*She laughs. She goes to get the paper.*) What's showing? It'll say in the . . . Where's –?

She sees the paper. Ann stands and heads off.

Peter Where are you –?

Ann I have a headache. I'm going to lie down. (*She starts to leave, stops.*) Vi?

Vi turns to her.

Peter's not a little boy anymore. I don't think we should walk around like that in front of him.

She goes. Vi smiles, then looks at Peter and smiles, then as she looks through the paper, she rather self-con-sciously puts her blouse on and begins to button it.

SCENE FOUR

That night.
  Vi sits at the upright slightly out-of-tune piano, playing as the others sing. The others now include Hugh (late for-ties) and his daughter Rose (19). Betty is in the kitchen.

All (*singing*)
  The Bells of St Mary's
  I hear they are calling
  The young loves
  The true loves
  Who come from the sea.

  And so my beloved
  When red leaves are falling
  The love bells shall ring out
  Ring out for you and me.

They finish, but Hugh, who has been standing and singing enthusiastically, starts one more chorus – alone. Vi plays for him. He has an OK voice, though obvi-ously thinks it is a very fine one.

Hugh (*singing*)
   The Bells of St Mary's
   I hear they are calling (*He sits on the piano bench next
   to Vi and looks at her and smiles as he sings.*)
   The young loves (*He puts a hand on Vi's shoulder.*)
   The true loves
   Who come from the sea.

   *Vi, without missing a beat, pushes his hand off her
   shoulder.*

   And so my beloved
   When red leaves are falling (*He gestures for all to join
   in.*)

All (*singing*)
   The love bells shall ring out

   *Peter tries to catch Ann's eye, but she won't look at
   him.*

(*singing*)
   Ring out for you and me!

   *As they finish, Hugh laughs and applauds the others –
   they laugh and applaud as well.
      Mike, who has been holding a tray of drinks, begins
   passing them out. When Hugh gets his, he raises it to
   Peter:*

Hugh And Pete, my boy – welcome home to England!

Peter (*under his breath, correcting*) Peter.

All Welcome home!

   *Those who don't have glasses reach for one, and the
   'welcome home' sort of peters out around spilling
   drinks, clinking glasses, etc.*

Ann And how we've missed him.

Peter suddenly turns to Ann, who turns away. Betty enters from the kitchen carrying a cake.

Betty Did I hear 'welcome home'?!

Reactions from the others: 'Look at this!' 'Oh my God!' 'It's beautiful!' 'A cake!' etc.

(*over this*) Four eggs went into this!

Vi (*explaining*) We pooled our coupons.

Betty It's just out of the oven.

Others smell.

Peter (*touched*) Thank you.

Betty It was Ann's idea.

Peter turns to Ann, hesitates.

Vi Go ahead and hug her. She's not going to bite.

Peter gives Ann a gentle hug of thank you.

(*to the others*) Why are men like that with pregnant women? They think they're going to break them?

She laughs. Ann smiles, first at Peter, then at the others.

Mike (*about the cake*) Why are you showing him now? We haven't eaten.

Vi As if he couldn't smell it.

Mike What happened to surprises?

Betty We've had enough surprises.

Hugh (*over some of this*) A cake! So now we start to have cakes again! Now there's a sign that it's all over.

Mike I think it's just a cake.

Hugh I haven't even *seen* four eggs together since –.

40

Things are back the way they used to be!

Betty (*to Ann, over this*) Is that what a cake means?

Ann shrugs.

I'd better take it back.

Vi (*standing*) I can do that. Sit down, Betty.

Betty Supper will be ready – in ten minutes.

Vi takes the cake from Betty.

Peter (*to Betty*) Beautiful cake. Really.

Betty (*pinching his cheek*) For my baby.

Hugh (*to Vi as she starts for the kitchen*) I'm sorry about – putting my arm on . . . I didn't mean . . . It must have been a – reflex?

He smiles at her. This has got the attention of the room. Vi says nothing and leaves for the kitchen.

Mike What did you do?

Hugh At the piano, I touched her shoulder. She flinched –. You'd think I'd . . . (*Laughs.*) I didn't mean –.

Betty (*suddenly grabs his hand and puts it on her shoulder*) Here. You can put it here. (*She laughs.*) All of us don't mind.

Others laugh. She wears her new blouse – without bra. Hugh catches a quick look down her blouse.

Hugh Nice blouse.

Betty (*turns to Peter and says a little too loud*) See!

Peter (*to Ann, confused*) See what?

Ann (*ignoring Peter*) All he gave me was a necklace.

She is wearing it. Rose turns and looks at it and smiles.
Beat. Then, as Vi is out of the room:

Hugh She's a charming girl, Vi.

Mike She is.

Hugh Plays the piano – very nicely. (*Turns to Betty,
whom he is still holding.*) She's the youngest?

Peter No, I am.

Hugh (*to Betty*) An actress too? I can see that.

Betty Why are we talking about Vi?

Ann (*to Rose*) What about you, Rose, any brothers or
sisters?

*Rose shakes her head. Hugh grabs her and hugs her –
she barely lets him.*

Hugh (*hugging Rose*) All alone in the world, poor baby.
(*As he hugs her, turns to Peter.*) So you were gone – five
years?

Peter Nearly six.

Hugh (*still hugging Rose*) My God, will our children ever
forgive us?

Mike (*sipping his drink*) What choice was there? So what
is there to forgive us for?

Betty (*looking at Peter*) Still – look at how well he's
turned out. Except for the accent! (*Smiling, she goes to
Peter.*) And we'll get rid of that!! (*She starts tickling him.*)

Peter (*trying to get away*) Betty, stop it! Stop! Ann!

Ann doesn't move.

Rose I think he sounds like a movie star.

Betty A movie star!! Oh that's even worse!! (*She tickles him even more.*)

Hugh (*over this, nodding to Rose*) Her mother ran off with an American.

This quiets Betty.

(*to Rose*) When was this? (*He smiles.*)

Rose You know very well.

Hugh (*continues*) August '43. A journalist. He comes to talk to me about the demands of surgery. At home. What we have to cope with. I told him – we work twelve-hour days. 'Don't you even come home for tea?' he asks. 'No, sir. Not these days.' Then for some reason – I come home for tea – and guess who's in bed with her mother? (*He laughs.*) So there he is, trying to put on his trousers and he's shouting at me: 'You lied to me! You lied to the Press!'

Laughter. Perhaps Hugh laughs a little too hard.

Betty (*laughing, still a little giddy*) Father would have liked that. (*to Rose*) He was a journalist.

Hugh (*to Rose*) She's where now? I always forget.

Rose No, you don't.

Hugh Cleveland, Ohio. I found a magazine with some pictures. Looks like a God-forsaken place. (*Shrugs.*) But I'm sure she's right at home.

Short pause.

Rose (*quietly*) That's not how it happened.

Vi comes out of the kitchen, everyone turns to her.

Vi (*confused*) What??

Rose (*graciously*) You're an actress, I understand. You

43

sing and play wonderfully well.

Vi smiles, but is still a little confused why she is the centre of attention.

Betty She was almost in *Autumn Fire*.

Rose Which one –?

Hugh (*interrupting*) Rose sings. (*Beat.*) Sing.

Rose Father –.

Hugh Like a bird. And dances. (*Turns to Peter.*) When she was a kid, she used to pull up her skirt and really kick like she'd seen in the pictures. It was the sweetest thing –. And sexy. (*to Rose, smiling*) I can say that now.

Rose Father –.

Peter I'm sure.

Hugh (*over this, continuing*) Now she's going to be a teacher. And that's very clever, isn't it?

Peter (*being polite*) How interesting –.

Hugh (*over him, to Ann*) You know you've got lots of company, don't you?

Ann (*confused*) Company? What . . .?

Hugh (*to the room*) I don't think a day goes by –. (*Turns to Mike.*) Does it?

Mike I don't know what you're –.

Hugh (*continuing*) – without two, three, sometimes five even six women coming in – pregnant.

Ann I do know two or –.

Hugh (*not listening*) It's like a – what's the word I'm looking for?

44

Peter Plague?

Others laugh, then Peter laughs.

Hugh (*laughing*) No! Anyway, I figure – and I've talked about this with Rose – and I think she's listened – it's teachers that are really going to be needed now. Someone to take care of all these bloody babies. (*Beat.*) It's *the* field right now.

Betty Sounds like it.

Hugh And Rose has got it worked out so . . . Tell them.

Rose (*embarrassed*) Tell them what, Father?

Hugh That if – you – how it's not a waste . . .

Rose (*biting the bullet*) If I study to be a teacher and – and I get married, then well I haven't really wasted my time. I can put what I've learned into helping my own children.

Hugh (*rubs her head*) Clever, isn't she? And realistic. Did you know that there are nearly two girls for every boy right now? (*to Peter*) Maybe you shouldn't be hearing this. (*He laughs.*) For every healthy boy. So you've got to be realistic. (*Beat.*) Betty's realistic.

Betty Am I?

Hugh I've seen you at Mike's side. He'd better be careful or I'll steal you away! (*Laughs.*)

Betty (*over the laughter*) Please, steal me away!

More laughter. She catches Mike's eye.

Mike (*joining in the 'joking'*) You'll have to fight me first!

Betty (*smiling*) Is that really true?

The laughter subsides, then:

Mike Seriously, Betty's a fine nurse. Any surgeon would be lucky to have her at his side. (*He looks at Betty, then 'presents her'.*) And she cooks!

Peter laughs, thinking this is still the joking, but no one else does. Suddenly the conversation has taken a more serious tone.

Hugh I'm looking forward to supper. (*Turns to Betty.*) And that is a very handsome blouse.

Betty Thank you.

Mike She manages the whole household. Doesn't she?

He turns to Ann and Vi, who say nothing.

Betty And I keep the books.

Peter (*confused*) What is –?

Ann Sh-sh.

She hits him to be quiet. Hugh stares at Betty, who stands perfectly still.

Hugh (*finally*) And you're the oldest.

Betty nods.

Usually the oldest is the most responsible. Most trustworthy.

Mike When Ann and Vi returned from Wales – Betty was like their mother. She did everything. (*He looks Betty over again.*)

Hugh I can't believe you wouldn't miss her, Mike.

Mike I know I would.

Short pause.

Betty (*finally*) Dinner should be ready. Excuse me. (*She goes off to the kitchen.*)

Peter (*half-whisper to Ann*) Isn't he going to look at her teeth?

Ann Sh-sh!

Mike (*to Hugh, as he fills his glass*) Always the responsible one. She runs the surgery for me, Hugh. There are days when I think why did I even bother to come in.

Beat.

Rose Are you looking for a nurse, Father?

No response. Suddenly Hugh turns his attention to Vi:

Hugh But you – you are a wonderful singer. And I love – to sing. As you probably figured out.

Vi (*barely hiding the lie*) And you sing very well.

Hugh Thank you.

Rose If a little too loudly.

They laugh. Hugh turns back to Vi.

Hugh You sing. You play. You act?

Vi Yes. (*She stands, feeling awkward, caught in his stare.*)

Ann When we were at school, Vi won third prize for her singing.

Hugh Only third prize?

Vi This was in Wales.

Hugh Of course. What sort of plays do you like to act in?

Vi doesn't know how to answer.

I've always thought that backstage in a theatre must be one of the most – I don't know – there must be a real kind of excitement. Of life. Actors rushing around, changing costumes – right off the stage, I'm told –. Waiting.

47

Anticipating. Then! (*Slaps his hands.*) I've had two patients who were actresses. I know something about acting.

He stares at her, then she goes and sits. He turns to Ann.

And you, Ann, we haven't said a word about you.

Ann I don't think Mike will let you steal me away.

Laughter.

Will you?

More laughter.

Hugh (*looking at her*) I haven't delivered enough babies. I should deliver more. (*Beat.*) They're inducing more and more now, aren't they, Mike? It's so much easier to schedule that way. You go from one to the next, I'm told. And it's even safer for the mother, isn't it?

Mike As soon as her waters break, we plan to induce.

Vi (*to Ann*) Do you know about this –?

Ann Mike's told me what to expect.

Mike Which isn't much. We'll put her under. She won't feel a thing. She won't even know what's happening to her.

He takes Ann's hand and squeezes it. Hugh suddenly turns to Peter.

Hugh Pete, Rose here is also a very good cook.

Rose Daddy!

Peter That's [nice] –.

Hugh And smart as a whip.

He points to her head. Betty suddenly bursts out of the kitchen, wearing Peter's cowboy hat, and announces:

Betty Dinner is served!

*The others react to the hat: 'What's that?' 'Peter's!'
'Take it off.'*

Hugh (*as they are going, to Betty*) That's what I imagine
my wife wearing now.

Rose I don't think they wear cowboy hats in Cleveland,
Ohio.

Vi Is that where she –?

*Hugh suddenly interrupts by putting his arm around Vi
and whispering something.*

Go ahead, if you want.

Mike stops Peter.

Mike Peter, can you help me collect the glasses.

*As the others head off, Hugh breaks into another cho-
rus of 'The Bells of St Mary's'. Only Betty joins in.
They are off.*
    Peter starts to collect the glasses.

Do you like Rose?

This stops Peter.

You don't mind that she's here.

Peter Why would I mind?

Mike Good. She's just a little older than you, I think. But
probably not nearly as – experienced?

*He tries to smile, Peter looks at him, is about to say
something, when:*

(*biting his nail*) Ann talked to me about this morning.

Beat.

Peter What about this morning??

Mike (*seemingly changing the subject*) Today in surgery
there was Mrs Jones. She was with her husband – Mr
Jones. (*Smiles at the obviousness of this and continues.*)
She's been fainting. Dizzy. You could see the disease in her
eyes, Peter. They both looked at me, expecting. Hopeful.
This man had served his country. (*Beat.*) I knew she was
dying. I could have told them this. (*Beat.*) They could
have spent the next – months? Building memories? I could
have begun this for them. But instead, I said – something
like – 'Your wife, Mr Jones, has a thirty to forty per cent
chance of extending normalcy through this year.' 'Thirty
to forty per cent?' I heard him say. 'Better than we had
hoped.' Translated, what I said meant – she might maybe
live through the remainder of this year – these next seven
months, but probably not. But they heard something different. I'm a coward, Peter. I can't . . . It's not in my
nature, I think . . . Don't hate me for that. (*He smiles – at
his own exaggeration. Then, holding out his arm*) That's
me! Now you know me!

*He smiles. The singing from the kitchen has stopped.
Ann appears.*

Ann Mike? Peter?

Mike In a minute.

*Peter looks at Ann, who returns to the kitchen. From
where we start to hear 'The White Cliffs of Dover'.
Mike sighs, this is obviously very difficult for him. He
sighs again, then:*

She told me about seeing you in the bath and what that
made her feel, Peter. (*He tries to smile.*) And then you sent
her back to her room. Thank you. A child's punishment
for a child's . . . (*Beat.*) Good for you. And that is what
happened.

50

Peter Are you telling me –?

Mike And that is what happened. (*He stares at Peter, then:*) Women when they are pregnant, Peter – I speak as a doctor – well they don't always do the rational thing. That's an understatement. (*Smiles.*) So it's up to us. To help them out. Not let their – emotions – get the best of them. (*Beat.*) She was embarrassed when she told me. Even contrite. Now I suspect she's forgotten the whole thing. As should you. As will you. (*Suddenly a big smile*) Come here! Here. (*Grabs him and holds his head.*) God, I know this can't be easy. But know that you have me. All right? Anytime you want to talk. Need an ear. (*Steps back, holds open his arms as he did before.*) That's me!

Vi (*off*) Mike!!

Mike Coming!! (*Slaps Peter's shoulder.*) I'll get Rose to help you with those . . . [the glasses].

Peter I don't need any –.

Mike She's a good-looking girl.

He winks and goes. Peter picks up a few glasses. Rose appears.

Rose I'm supposed to help . . .

From the kitchen we hear: 'Are we eating?' 'Start serving,' etc.

Are those all the glasses?

He hands her one.

Thanks. I suppose we should take them back in the kitchen. (*Beat.*) Do you ever go to the pictures? I love the pictures. I never say no to anyone who asks me to go to the pictures.

Peter hesitates, then, without saying a word, heads for

the kitchen. Rose, a little hurt, follows.
    *Off we hear their arrival: 'At last!' 'Now can we eat?'
etc.*
    *And the scooting of chairs being moved around the
table, the murmur of talk. Then the clinking of a glass
as Mike tries to get everyone's attention for grace.*

Mike (*off*) Dear God, Father of us all, we ask You to
bless this our table and we, Your children . . .

SCENE FIVE

Later that night.
    *Radio is on – the glow of the yellow dial is the only
light visible. Ann sits alone, curled up in a chair, smoking.*
    *Noise off, footsteps, voices, etc. Door to the outside
hallway opens – Vi, Betty, Peter and Mike enter talking.*

Vi (*teasing*) Come on. Come on, Betty! Say what you
think of him! (*to the others*) She won't say. Why won't
she say?

Peter (*to Ann*) You're sitting in the dark.

    They start turning on lights.

Vi Is he your type? Is he not your type?

Betty He's not my type.

Vi He's not her type.

    They are taking off their coats, etc.

Well I thought he was sort of good looking.

Betty I know you did.

Vi What is that supposed to mean?

    No response.

52

Ann (*to Mike*) What happened?

Vi (*continuing*) So – I think you're making a mistake.

Betty What sort of mistake am *I* making, Vi?

Mike (*to Ann*) About Hugh.

Vi A doctor. Not bad looking. Divorced. (*Still teasing, Vi winks at Peter.*)

Betty You don't know anything.

Vi (*smiling*) I think she fancies this man, that is exactly what I think.

Betty (*upset, but the others don't see this yet*) He's looking for a nurse! (*Turns to Mike.*) Did you know that? I couldn't just leave you.

Mike (*smiling*) You do what you want. (*Turns to the others and smiles. Leans over and kisses Ann on the head.*) How's the headache.

Ann I'm all right.

Betty (*erupts*) So I just do what I want?! I don't think I even know what that is anymore! I think I've forgotten even what that means!

Ann (*concerned*) Betty –.

Betty (*very upset now*) I think it's been beaten out of my skull! I think all I know now how to do is take care of people! Do what you want!!

   Vi suddenly smiles. Confused, she turns to Ann.

(*to Vi*) Go ahead and laugh at me!

Vi I wasn't laughing at –.

Betty (*then it comes out*) He was all over you, Vi.

Vi What??

Betty And you encouraged him!!

Vi I did no such thing.

Betty You selfish little girl. You've always been so selfish!

Ann Stop it, Betty! Stop it!

Betty (*over this*) I saw you crossing your legs. We're talking about something else and suddenly – it's legs. How he likes legs! (*Beat.*) I hate my legs. I hate them.

She starts to cry and runs off to her bedroom. The others are stunned, having had no idea how serious this was.

Ann What . . .?

Vi I did nothing. Nothing!

Ann Something must –.

Vi I think the guy's a joke. A moron. Why would I try and pick him up? (*Beat.*) She's insane. (*Shrugs.*) She shouldn't drink.

Peter She hardly drank anything.

Vi (*yelling*) Then I don't know what her problem is. Don't blame me!

Mike (*quietly*) She must have heard . . .

Vi What?

Beat.

Mike Hugh and I were talking –. I told him to – sh-sh. And Betty was walking back from the Ladies. He looked at her – he said he thought her ankles were thick. (*Beat.*) I didn't think she heard . . .

Ann He said that?

Mike (*making light of it*) We were looking at all the girls. Not just Betty. This one's nose is too small. This one's . . . you know. (*suddenly remembering*) He liked her breasts. He said – Betty's got nice breasts. But thick ankles. So it was sort of – balancing: this is good, this is not as good . . . (*Beat.*) He didn't mean anything by it. In his defence, he . . . (*Shrugs. Pause.*)

Ann She must like him.

Vi Not necessarily.

Ann True.

Suddenly the phone rings. They look at each other, then Vi picks it up.

Vi (*into phone*) Hello? Oh . . . I'll look. (*She covers the receiver.*) It's the tactful – Hugh. He's lost his hat, he wonders if he left it here.

They immediately see it on a table. All point. Vi starts to uncover the receiver, then has a better idea. She sets the phone down and goes to the hallway and calls.

Betty! Telephone! Betty! Betty!!

Betty appears, very hesitant.

It's – Hugh.

Betty starts to go back. Vi grabs her.

He's lost his hat. It's right over there. Tell him.

Betty tries to leave again, Vi holds her.

Tell him!

Suddenly her sister and brother see what Vi is doing and join in: 'Tell him, Betty! Please, Betty! Tell him! Tell him!' Even Mike joins in, but without really knowing what is going on. Ann, Vi and Peter plead: 'Betty!'

Betty finally goes to the phone, picks it up.

Betty Hello? . . . It's Betty. Your hat's here.

She starts to hang up. But Hugh has said something.

What? . . . Thank you. It was Mother's recipe actually . . . I'll write it down if you like and post it . . . What? (*Beat.*) Tomorrow? . . . Let me think. (*to the others*) Am I free tomorrow night?

The others just stare at her.

Yes, I think I am free. That would be very nice indeed. Thank you so much. Goodnight. (*She hangs up. Short pause.*) He asked me out. On a date. I think I'll do the washing up now. (*She turns and starts to go, then stops and speaks to Mike.*) He's a nice man. I like him. (*She smiles, turns to the others and tries to make a joke. Patting Mike*) And if I can't have Father here, then I'll have to settle for Hugh. (*Then she realizes what she has just said.*)

Peter (*quietly*) Father??

Betty (*embarrassed*) I mean – Mike. Mike here. I'm just joking Ann. (*She tries to laugh. Then, to say something*) He's taking me to dinner. Hugh.

She goes. No one says anything for a moment, then:

Vi I'll help Betty.

Mike What was all that about? Sometimes I walk into this house and I feel I don't have a clue about what's going on. (*He turns to Ann, and Peter near her.*)

Peter I should probably get to bed.

Vi (*goes to Peter*) Funny, your sisters, aren't they? (*She kisses him on the cheek.*) Thanks for taking me to the pictures.

Peter (*to Ann and Mike*) I'm sorry to report I didn't have to fight anyone off! (*He smiles.*)

Vi And thanks – for coming home. Goodnight. (*to Ann and Mike*) I'll help Betty do the washing up. 'Night.

Ann Goodnight.

Vi goes into the kitchen.

Vi (*off, to Betty*) So I'm a selfish little girl, am I?

Betty (*off*) I'm sorry, I didn't mean –.

Vi I'm joking, I know –.

Door closes and we don't hear any more.

Ann (*to Mike*) I won't be long.

Mike I'll get myself another –.

Ann You've had enough to drink. Go to bed. Peter can keep me company.

Peter is surprised by this. Mike looks at him. Nods, then:

Mike I'll read. (*He goes.*)

Ann I think he has a girlfriend. His nurse. (*Beat.*) What do you think?

Peter shrugs and goes to the bottle on the tray.

What are you doing?

Peter I want a drink.

Ann You're seventeen years old! And I don't know what Mike is doing taking you to a pub –.

She tries to take the bottle away, Peter holds it out of her reach.

Peter Father gave me my first drink years ago. Right in this room.

Ann What are you talking about –?

Peter I was ten, I think.

Ann suddenly realizes.

Ann Oh my God, are you drunk?!

Peter (*over this*) He poured me a beer. Then another. Then a third and I threw up. He said, son – if you're going to drink, then I want you to learn how to drink, right here in your home. (*Beat.*) Well, I'm home. (*He pours himself a drink. Beat. Points towards the kitchen.*) Maybe I should help.

No response. He sits.

I want to go to bed. (*He sips his drink.*) Why did you talk about this morning with Mike?

Ann Because . . . (*Shrugs.*) he's my husband? I don't know. (*Beat.*) But I didn't tell him what happened. Because nothing happened, Peter. We have to face that. Accept that. (*Beat.*) Mike was terribly interested – in my feelings. He was almost sweet about it. (*Beat.*) I think it was the doctor in him.

Peter (*interrupting*) I could have stopped you, this morning, you know.

Ann Stop what? What happened? You sent me to my room. A naughty, naughty girl. (*suddenly*) It was a dream! I'm not a freak! I hate it that you're drinking by the way. I really hate it.

He sets down his glass.

So – how was little – what's-her-name?

Peter Who?

Ann Hugh's –.

Peter Rose.

Ann I knew it was some – form of vegetation. (*Beat.*) She was a late addition to the night, did you know? Mike asked Hugh to bring her along for you. (*Beat.*) After our talk –. His conclusion was that you needed a date. Did you know that she was your date?

Peter Yes.

Ann Oh. (*Beat.*) I look at you and see a ten-year-old boy. I've got to get used to this. I thought she was dear. Sort of. Maybe you should ask her out. Or maybe you have? I've got a little pocket money, you could take her to the pictures. She obviously likes the pictures. Let me give it to you . . .

She gets out of the chair and goes to get her purse. Peter stops her, holds her arm. She shakes him off.

No.

Peter suddenly erupts.

Peter What game are you playing with me?!

Beat.

Ann No game. None. (*She stares at him.*) I'm trying to be – good. I'm trying to close my eyes and say: 'Mother, please tell me what to do?' (*Beat.*) There is no one in the world I'd rather hold – than you. To hug. To touch. I want you pressed against me. Breathing each breath with me. (*Beat.*) I see the boy. I see – the brother. I see the man. Like pages in a book flicking by – faster and faster. Never stopping. All blurring into the next, Peter. All – at the same time. (*Beat.*) I love you so much.

Short pause.

Peter And what does Mother say?

Laughter from the kitchen. Ann looks at him, then shrugs. Peter leans over and kisses her on the cheek.

Ann Tell me – was that a brotherly kiss? Or . . . Tell me, Peter, because otherwise I should hit you. Should I hit you? (*Suddenly turns away.*) Remember having to line up in the kitchen, when we'd all done something wrong? Mother had that big wooden spoon. Where was Father?

Peter Probably drunk.

Ann Probably on business. (*continuing:*) You were the youngest. So you were the last. And by then Mother would always say, 'Now I think I've made my point.' She couldn't strike you. Her daughters – no problem.

Peter I remember being hit –.

Ann By us! We hit you, Peter! We took you out into the garden and gave you a good beating!

She laughs. Betty and Vi come out of the kitchen, laughing, the best of pals now.

Betty We're leaving the rest till morning. And I don't care if that's a sin! (*noticing Ann and Peter smiling*) What??

Vi They were always the closest.

Betty That is true, isn't it.

Vi I used to be jealous.

Peter (*explaining*) Ann was telling me how you'd take me out to the garden –.

Ann (*same time*) When Mother wouldn't hit him! With his cricket bat!

Peter Cricket bat?

Vi Betty held you down.

Betty I was the strongest!

Vi And I made a little mark with my fingernail on the bat. For every smack –.

Betty You hated that so we kept doing it.

Peter I don't remember the bat.

Vi I'm sure it's here somewhere. This family throws nothing away. (*to Betty*) Do we?

Betty (*to Ann*) By the way, I'm sorry about earlier . . .

Ann Please.

Vi (*going up to Peter as if to kiss him on the cheek*) Goodnight. (*She suddenly tickles him.*)

Betty He was always a sucker. Goodnight little brother!

Peter Goodnight.

They are halfway down the hall.

Ann (*calling*) I'm going to bed too!

Vi and Betty are gone. Peter and Ann are again alone. Pause.

(*then, as if picking up the old conversation:*) Anyway, I'm ugly. A handsome boy like you – why would you want me?

Peter looks at her.

Peter You're the most beautiful woman I know.

Short pause.

Ann Have you ever had a girlfriend?

Peter hesitates, then shaking his head:

Peter No.

Short pause.

Ann Not even – 'Auntie Fay'?

Peter (*seriously*) Stop it.

Ann Sorry. It was a joke. Come here. Come here.

Peter approaches her. Stops.

Peter Are you going to tickle me?

Ann smiles, and shakes her head. She takes his head and presses it against hers. She kisses his cheek, his ear, his neck, then looks at him.

Ann At least I have better legs than Betty.

This suddenly makes them both laugh, and equally suddenly this laugh turns into a passionate kiss. They pull away, breathless.

I'll come to your room with you.

Peter But –.

Ann Mike's asleep. I'm sure he's asleep. (*Beat.*) I'll just check.

She hurries towards her bedroom, leaving Peter alone. He waits, touches his face, sighs, bites his nails. Then, after a long pause, Ann returns.

(*without looking at Peter*) Mike wants another drink.

She pours a drink and exits.

The next morning.
  Peter, barefoot, but dressed, sits on the sofa, pretending to read his book.

Betty (*off, from her bedroom*) Vi!!! I hate this! I look like I don't know what! Vi!!!

  Vi comes out of the kitchen.

Vi I'm coming . . .

  Mike is right behind her, he holds his teacup.

Mike Will you tell her we have to go –?

Betty (*off*) Vi, help me!

Vi (to *Mike*) Tell her yourself –.

Mike (*over this*) Betty!! We have to –!!

  Betty enters from the bedroom. She wears one of Vi's tight-fitting dresses.

Betty (*entering*) I can't even bend over in . . . (*She tries, stops.*)

Mike I like it!

Betty I'm not going to believe a word you say.

  She smiles. Mike laughs.

Mike (*'innocently'*) Why not? (*He laughs and winks at Peter.*)

Betty (*turns to Vi, about the dress*) Look, you can actually see the crease in my bottom.

  Mike 'leans over and looks' and winks at Peter.

Vi Is that bad?

Betty (*over this*) I can't walk in it. What else have you got? (*She heads for the bedrooms.*)

Mike Betty, we have to go to work! Can't you do that –?

Betty When? I get off at six. (*Turns back to Vi.*) In this he'll think I'm a bloody whore.

Vi (*as she and Betty go*) I very much doubt that.

Vi and Betty are gone.

Mike (*to Peter*) Extraordinary. In the surgery – she's like a rock.

He looks at his watch. Ann has entered in her dressing gown.

There she is! Sleeping Beauty awakens! (*to Peter*) There's something to be said for a house full of women, isn't there? (*back to Ann*) She walks. She talks. Or does she?

Ann Good morning. (*She kisses Mike on the cheek as she passes him. She goes to the sofa. To Peter*) Is there room there?

Peter moves and she sits down.

(*to Peter*) Morning.

Mike Cup of tea?

Peter (*starting to stand*) I'll get you one.

Ann (*stopping him*) No, no, please. I don't want anything.

Peter sits back down. Ann pats his knee.

How did you sleep?

Betty and Vi burst back into the room. Betty is now in

64

her underwear, she holds a blue dress in front of her. Vi holds another dress.

Betty Ann, which do you think, the blue or the green?

Mike Betty, I'm leaving in two minutes.

Peter Wasn't the blue one Mother's?

This stops everyone for a moment.

Betty Was it?

Peter I'm pretty sure.

Vi I think it was, he's right.

Beat.

Betty Then it's the blue one. Mother would have liked that.

Vi The hem's too low though. (*She leans down and pulls up the hem, revealing more and more of Betty's leg.*) How's this? (*higher, teasing*) How's this?

Betty Stop it!

Vi He'd like it like that. We know he likes legs.

Others laugh, Betty pretends she didn't hear it.

Betty (*to Peter*) You really remember Mother in this?

Peter I think so.

Betty sighs, presses the dress against her chest and starts to head back to her bedroom. As she turns, Vi notices a hole in Betty's underpants.

Vi Betty, you can't wear . . . (*She sticks her finger in the hole.*)

Betty (*hitting her hand away*) What are you doing?

Vi (*sticking her finger back in the hole*) There's a hole. You can't wear these –.

Betty He's not going to see my –.

Mike (*over this, turning*) I'm not watching!

Vi (*over this, to Betty*) Are you so sure of that?!

    Betty hurries out of the room.

(*to the room*) Really, it's like dressing a child. (*She follows Betty off.*)

Mike (*calls*) I'm going, Betty! Tell her I've gone.

    He goes to the sofa, leans down and kisses Ann on the head. She rubs his arm with her hand.

(*to Ann*) I forgot to tell you, Hugh mentioned last night that there might be a flat available in his building. I'll try and find out more.

    Ann freezes.

Peter What?

Mike Ann and I have been looking for our own –.

Ann No we haven't. Not for months.

Mike We just didn't find any –.

Ann We decided to stop looking. We liked it here –.

Mike (*over this*) We need our own flat!

    Suddenly Ann and Mike are shouting at each other.

Ann My sisters are here and my brother!

Mike Your sisters could have their own rooms!

Ann And when the baby's born –.

Mike That's my point!

Ann – to have aunts and an uncle – to help, Mike!

Mike I'm going to look at the flat!!

Ann (*waving her arms, gesturing to this flat*) And who'll pay for –!!?

Mike I will pay, dammit!!!

Pause. Mike looks at Peter, who turns away.

Ann This is an important conversation, we just can't –.

Mike I have to go.

Ann You're always doing this –.

Mike Goodbye.

He goes. Short pause. Betty hurries out of the bedroom, now in her nurse's uniform.

Betty Where's –? (*She looks around, realizes Mike is gone.*) Bye. Goodbye. See you tonight.

She quickly kisses Peter on the top of the head, touches Ann's shoulder and hurries out after Mike. We hear her footsteps down the steps.
  Vi appears in the doorway.

Vi She's like dressing a doll. She has that much knowledge of clothes.

Ann Well, I'm sure you helped . . .

Vi I tried. I did my best. (*She starts to put on a jumper.*)

Ann Where are you going?

Vi Into town. They might be filming that picture in Leicester Square. It's not raining today. (*Beat.*) You two going to be OK?

Peter Yes. I think so.

Vi Don't wait on her, Peter. She's stronger than she looks. And she's more than capable of taking advantage. I can swear to that.

Ann (*smiling*) Be quiet.

Peter (*smiling*) I'll – be careful.

Vi goes to the door, stops.

Vi You don't feel I'm abandoning you, do you?

Peter You have to work. And Ann's here. And we did go to the pictures yesterday.

Vi True. That's true.

Ann Now it's my turn – to be with him.

Vi Right. Good. See you later then. (*And she is gone, leaving Peter and Ann alone on the sofa.*)

Ann (*quietly*) Bye. (*She turns to Peter, then turns away and stands.*) So . . . I hate Mike.

Peter looks at her.

You heard him. Sometimes I hate him. And sometimes I say to myself, you shouldn't stay with someone you hate. And I believe that. (*Shrugs. She picks up Mike's teacup.*) Tea?

Peter shakes his head. Ann starts to head off for the kitchen, then returns right away.

Father used to do that to me. (*Beat.*) I remember once, he had a taxi waiting. I helped him down with his bag. He let me. He helped me help him. And as he was getting in – after a glance at the ticking meter? He said, 'Ann, I've decided which school you're going to.' Then taxi door slam and he was gone. No discussion. Nothing. (*Beat.*) Like you're a – thing to be told. Like you are nothing.

68

(*Beat.*) I'm going to clean today. You can help me. Move the chairs around, that sort of thing. (*Short pause.*) It's because of you that Mike's looking for another flat. Suddenly we're – 'crowded'. (*Beat.*) All I ask is for the opportunity to talk about things. Before decisions are made. Before things are done, and can't be – reversed. (*She looks at Peter.*) You are so young. I can't believe how young you are. (*Beat.*) So what are we going to do today? Should we talk about it? (*Short pause.*) I love this flat. I must know every inch. (*Pointing to the sofa*) I remember – God knows how old I was – certainly not old enough to 'get it' – but I came around that corner. And there was Mother and Father on that sofa. Right there, Peter. Her blouse was – it was hanging off her shoulder. She was sitting on Dad. (*Beat.*) The upholstery is the same as it was then. We haven't changed it. (*Beat.*) I'm not going to the pictures with you. I've stopped all that. You can go yourself if you want. (*Short pause. She thinks, then:*) You step outside today – just one foot out of your home – and it all makes no sense anymore. And it's been building up to this for a while. (*Suddenly remembers.*) About a month ago, I was out –. You know the shop – it used to be a greengrocer's near the surgery on the High Street? Of course you don't know it. Well, it's reopened. And do you know what they're selling – the only thing they are selling as far as I could tell? Crows. Dead crows. Rows and rows and rows of hanging black crows. They're selling them – to eat, I think. (*Beat.*) Go and have a look if you like. Quite a sight. (*Short pause. She comes and sits next to him, takes his hand, puts it on her stomach.*) It's kicking. (*Her mind drifts away, to:*) You try and make sense –. You start to ask yourself – should I do this? Should I do that? (*Beat.*) You have such a wonderful smell about you. (*She takes his hand and holds it.*) We're all alone. (*Pause. She suddenly stands.*) I need to go for a pee. Excuse me.

She goes off down the hallway to the bedrooms and
W.C.
    Peter is alone. He sits, nearly frozen.
    Ann returns, tying her dressing gown.

Walking past your room, I noticed you haven't made your
bed, Peter. (*Beat.*) If you'd like, I could make it. (*Beat.*)
Could I make it? (*Beat.*) I'll go and make your bed, Peter.

She goes off down the hallway to his bedroom. Peter
watches her go, stands, and follows her out.

SCENE SEVEN

Early evening.
    Peter sits on the sofa, his book in his lap.
    There is a knock on the door. Peter does not respond.
Another knock.

Vi (*off*) Is that the door? Peter, will you get it?!

Peter does not move. Another knock.

Peter?!

Another knock. Vi hurries on from the bedrooms.

Did you hear the door?!

Suddenly it is like Peter 'comes to' – he really hadn't
heard it.
    Vi opens the door, and there is Hugh, flowers in
hand.

Hugh May I come in?

Vi Please, of course. Betty will be –. Shall I take those?
(*the flowers*)

Hugh (*joking*) They're not for you.

70

Vi (*embarrassed*) I know. I meant –.

Hugh laughs a little too loudly.

Hugh And where is that beautiful sister of yours –?

Vi She'll be out in –.

Ann, dressed now, appears in the kitchen doorway.

Hugh (*seeing Ann and pointing*) There she is! (*He laughs.*)

Ann Peter, get Hugh a drink. He's a man in need of a drink. You remember Peter.

Hugh (*over this*) I'm teasing.

Vi I'll tell Betty you're here.

She goes. Peter has got up and goes to the drinks.

Hugh (*as if explaining, to Peter*) I have four sisters. (*He smiles.*)

Peter Whisky?

Hugh (*nods, then:*) Where's Mike –? Is he –?

Ann Not home yet. Any minute, I suppose.

Hugh (*looking at his watch*) I'm impressed. He's working –.

Ann Let me get you something to have with your drink.

She goes into the kitchen, leaving Peter and Hugh alone. Peter hands Hugh his drink.

Hugh (*sips, then nods towards where Ann exited*) When's the baby – due?

Peter I don't know. (*Short pause. Peter sits back on the sofa.*)

Hugh He'll be a wonderful father.

Peter Good.

Hugh With some men – you can't tell. Me – I did my best. You saw my best. But it's a winnerless race raising a child. As I used to tell my ex-wife – the goal seems to be – to cause the least harm you can. (*Sips.*) He's a good man. Mike. Much admired. I understand he pays for all this –.

Peter I know.

Hugh Everything. (*Beat.*) And now you too. Ann's a lucky woman.

Peter And you're a lucky man.

This confuses Hugh. He half-smiles.

Hugh How so?

Peter Betty. She's the smartest of all us –.

Hugh (*seriously*) It's a date. (*Shrugs.*) Don't make too much out of it. You understand, I'm sure.

Beat.

Peter (*continuing*) The smartest, cleverest. She was the only one of us who was ever able to finish anything. She finished school. I'm sure she's a great nurse –.

Hugh But what about those ankles? (*He smiles.*)

Peter (*erupting*) For Christ sake – she's not a piece of meat!!

Hugh I'm teasing. I'm teasing you, Peter. If we can't take a joke anymore . . . I told you – four sisters. (*Beat.*) Sorry.

Ann comes out with a tray with biscuits.

Ann What were you two –?

Peter Hugh has four sisters.

Ann My condolences. And how is your lovely daughter? (*She turns to Peter for help.*)

Peter Rose.

Ann Rose. I love that name.

Peter (to *Hugh*) She wasn't scarred by the divorce?

Both Hugh and Ann are surprised by the question.

By your wife leaving you – for that American? The one you found in your wife's bed? (*Beat. Smiles.*) I'm just teasing.

Hugh Ask her. (*to Ann*) Boys love her, as you can guess.

Peter Was your divorce difficult? I suppose what I'm really asking is – was it expensive? (*He glances at Ann, then back to Hugh.*)

Hugh Not terribly. We decided most things before even talking to a solicitor.

Peter And that made it – less expensive?

Hugh Yes.

Peter again looks at Ann. Vi bursts in.

Vi Hugh, here she comes!

Betty enters in her mother's blue dress, hem raised to the knee, looking great. No one says anything for a moment, then:

Hugh You look great.

Nervous laughter.

Betty (*seeing the flowers*) Are those for me? (*She takes them, kisses Hugh on the cheek.*) Thank you. (*to Vi*)

Would you put them in water for me?

Vi takes the flowers.

(*to Hugh*) Where are you taking me?

Hugh (*shrugs, then:*) A drink first at the corner at the King's Head? Then – dinner?

Betty (*making a joke*) At the King's Head?!

Hugh No, no I didn't mean –.

Betty Sounds like fun. And then – after – we'll see.

The sisters react to this boldness: 'Ohhhhhh!' Hugh laughs nervously. Peter just watches.

Hugh I like this girl!

Betty (*holding up her jumper, to Hugh*) Would you mind?

Hugh helps her on with her jumper.

Should we go? Or do you want to finish that –? [the drink]

Hugh swallows the rest.

(*to Vi*) Goodnight. (*Kisses Vi.*) Goodnight, Ann. And baby. (*Kisses Ann.*) Goodnight. (*Kisses Peter.*)

Hugh Don't worry, she's in good hands. (*Laughs.*)

Peter Is that a joke too?

Vi (*over this, 'suddenly serious'*) Betty!

Betty What?

Vi quickly lifts up Betty's dress a bit. Betty, confused, pushes her hand away.

Vi Just making sure you're all dressed.

She laughs. Betty smiles at the joke. Everyone is saying 'Goodnight', 'Have a nice time', etc. The door is closed, they are gone, and immediately all the smiles disappear.

Peter Am I mad or did she look just like Mother?

Ann Just like her.

Vi nods. Pause. No one knows what to do. Ann starts rubbing her hands together.

Vi Are you all right?

Ann I'm fine –.

Vi Your hands are freezing.

Ann I'll just put another jumper on. (*She starts to go.*)

Peter (*to Ann*) That was interesting what he said about getting a divorce. It doesn't have to cost – everything.

Ann goes. Vi is confused by this, then turns to Peter.

Vi What a woman goes through to have a baby.

Peter Is that why she's –.

Vi I watch Ann and I think – never me. What about you? You want children?

Peter I haven't thought about it.

Vi Men don't, I find. Of course they have less reason to. Or need to – think about it. (*Beat.*) I loaned Betty a couple of French letters. She's a virgin, did you know that? Why would you? A virgin. She just told me. I couldn't believe it. I had to show her how to put them on. (*Holds up her finger and demonstrates.*) To make sure it was tight . . . You . . . (*Stops.*) You don't want to know about this. (*Beat.*) Twenty-one years old and still a . . . I asked her – why? There must be some reason she's had for waiting. Some – principle? Belief? No, she said. There was no reason.

Beat.

Peter So – Hugh????

Vi (*shrugs*) She said – she wondered if it was finally time to grow up.

Peter Grow up? Is that growing up? Is – Hugh –??

Ann enters with another jumper.

Ann (*entering*) What are we doing for supper? Anything?

Vi Sh-sh!!! We're in the middle of a very interesting conversation. (*She turns to Peter.*) Are you a virgin, Peter?

Ann Vi, you can't just ask –.

Vi (*over this*) If he doesn't want to answer, he doesn't have to.

Beat.

Peter No, no, I'm not a virgin.

Ann I think I'll go and begin a supper. (*She goes.*)

Vi She has no curiosity. (*Calls.*) If you need any help, just . . . (*Beat.*) She can't hear me. What about a drink? I need a drink. (*She gets up and goes to the drinks, stops.*) We should have asked if she [Ann] was a virgin.

She laughs. Peter smiles.

'Let me get you a drink, Father.' (*As she makes drinks.*) That's what Mother always said. 'Let me get –.' Explain something to me, why would a woman call her husband 'Father'? (*Beat.*) What did you do today?

Peter Nothing.

Vi (*not listening, handing him his drink*) 'Father'! Cheers. You spent all day here with Ann?

76

Peter Yes.

Vi Then you deserve that drink. Betty didn't even know how to put one on and she's a nurse! You look different today. Why do you look different?

No response.

You must have got some sleep. (*Beat.*) I got the part in *Autumn Fire*. The director changed his mind.

Peter Congratulations.

Vi (*over this*) That's good, isn't it? I'll have to be away for a while. On my own. You're the first to know.

Peter Vi, I love Ann.

Vi So do I. (*Beat.*) We're your sisters. You have to! (*Smiles.*) Not that it's always been –. (*touching her forehead*) I was looking in the mirror earlier, see this? (*Points to a spot on her forehead.*) See this little mark? You know how I got that? You, Petey –.

Peter Don't call me –.

Vi You hit me with a stone. I was maybe – four? Do you remember this?

Peter shakes his head.

Why should you. (*Beat.*) The scars we leave. (*She sits back.*) The first time I had sex –. Does this embarrass you?

Peter shakes his head.

Good. I was fifteen. He was a boy. Also from London. He hadn't seen his parents for – years too. We hung around. We played. When Ann wouldn't let me play with her friends. (*Beat.*) We did it outside. In the woods. I didn't have anything. No one told me about French letters. At

77

least not how to get one. We both were pretty frightened.
He was younger than me. Same as you. You'd like him, I
think. I don't know where he is now. (*Beat.*) Then that
afternoon – when I got back to the house from the
woods? A telegram was waiting for us. To tell us that
Mother had died. (*Beat.*) Guilty? Did I feel guilty, Peter?
The scars we leave. (*Beat.*) There is no greater curse on a
child, I believe, than to tie together once and for ever –
sex and death.

Pause.

Peter I mean – I love Ann as a woman.

Vi turns to him.

I love her body. I love to touch –.

*Vi suddenly slaps him hard across the face. He nearly
falls over.*

Vi Stop it! Stop it!! That's disgusting!!

Ann enters from the kitchen.

Ann What –?!

Vi (*making a 'joke'*) He got fresh. (*She tries to laugh.*)

Peter (*trying to lie*) I hit my head against . . . (*He looks to
find something he could have hit his head against.*)

Ann Against what?

Peter The sofa. The side of the sofa.

Ann How did you –?

Peter I was leaning and I –?

Ann Why were you leaning?

Peter I just hit it. That's all. I'm not sure how it happened. It was one of those – things.

Ann goes to him and looks at the bruise. She touches his face. Vi watches.

Vi Is the supper . . .?

Ann It needs to cook. (*She continues to touch Peter's face.*)

Peter I'm all right. I really am.

Vi Leave him alone.

Ann What?? (*She lets go of Peter.*)

Vi Leave our brother alone. He's not a child. We don't have to keep fawning over him.

They look at each other, then Vi turns away.

(*turning away*) Leave him alone. What were we talking about? The day Mother died. I was just talking about the day Mother died. I walk out of the woods, a little bloody, and Mum's dead. We're not the sisters you left. Are we, Ann? So much happened. There's so much Peter doesn't know about. So much he's missed. (*Beat.*) There was that woman. Weeks? Months later? After Mother's death, Father comes to visit us – with a woman. What was her name?

No response from Ann.

We never wrote to you about any of this. And the most remarkable thing was that she looked like Mother. Like a rather blurry carbon-copy of Mother. Wouldn't you agree?

Ann Exactly.

Peter looks at Ann.

Vi We look at her – we didn't know what to say. Father's got his arm around her. They hold hands. What am I to feel? Do I love her? Do I hate her? She tried – to be nice. At supper that night she was very nice. Then we went for a walk in the morning. Just 'us girls'. (*Beat.*) And we learned, didn't we, that she was obsessed with Mother. With things she'd heard – been told –.

Ann That Father was telling her –.

Vi Lies. How Mother had been so mean with some things –.

Ann Books, he told her.

Peter Mother was never mean with books –.

Vi (*over this*) And positively extravagant when it came to other things – for herself. Shoes. How many shoes?? That was not true! He was lying to her about Mother! Mother bought maybe three pairs of shoes at one time only because she had such narrow feet that when she found shoes that fitted her, which was rare! – she bought a few pairs! That makes sense. Doesn't it make sense?! That doesn't make her a spendthrift. That doesn't make her self-ish for God's sake!! She kept every damn shoe she ever bought and dyed them over and over and over! This wasn't our mother, woman! I know it sounds petty, but I can still see that face, that almost-mother's face, how I wanted to slap that face as she said, I remember every word, as she took my hand on that walk and said: 'It seems your mother wasn't a very kind woman. How hard that must have been for you. Still, I'm sure she tried to love you in her own way.' (*Short pause.*) We're weak, Peter. We've become very weak. (*to Ann*) Leave him alone.

Ann looks to Peter.

Peter I told her. She knows.

Ann nods. Peter turns to her, leans and kisses her on the mouth and fondles her breast. She lets him.

Vi (*covering her ears and closing her eyes, shouts*) No!!!!!!!

Silence.

Ann What else has he missed about our family, Vi? There's the letters. (*to Peter*) Why didn't he burn them? He was off to war, for God's sake! Letters to 'Father from women. Over years and years. (*Beat.*) Mother must have known.

Vi We disagree about that.

Ann I've read them. Vi's read them. Betty's so far refused. Just say when. (*She takes Peter's hand in hers.*)

Vi This is wrong. I hurt so much. (*Holds herself and whimpers:*) No. No. No.

Short pause.

Peter (*to Ann*) Vi got that part in that play. The director changed his mind.

Ann Good for you, Vi.

Vi I went to see the director today. At his flat. And slept with him. (*Beat. As a second thought*) The girl without –. (*Gestures.*) And her legs crossed? She had had the role.

Short pause.

Ann As Vi said – we're not the sisters you left.

Short pause.

Peter So poor Vi will have to be away from home for a while.

Short pause.

Ann Mike's looking at a new flat, Vi – for the baby. So I could be away from home too.

Door opens, Betty enters.

(*letting go of Peter's hand*) Betty, why are you –?

Vi (*same time*) Where's Hugh?

Betty looks at them and smiles. She is suddenly calm, not at all the flighty person she has been.

Betty I don't know. I just – left. I don't know what happened – it was like someone spoke to me and said: 'Look at this man, Betty. Have you looked at him?' (*Beat.*) So I did. And I saw – a nose I disliked. Talk about thick ankles – look at his nose. And hands – with all those hairs. And I hate his laugh. I hate his teasing. So why am I here? (*Beat.*) This isn't me. So I said I didn't feel well and came home. (*Turns to Ann.*) Ann, could you put the kettle on please.

Vi I'll do it –.

Betty Let Ann. She's always telling us not to wait on her.

Vi When has she said –?

Betty Sh-sh.

Ann (*getting up*) I'll put the kettle on. (*She goes.*)

Betty In the pub, Hugh got quite close to me and said, 'I hope this isn't difficult for you, but I've asked Mike to join us for dinner. I think he's bringing his other nurse.'

Ann returns.

Ann Kettle's on. (*Beat.*) We'll eat when Mike's home.

Betty (*picking up a framed photo*) I think it was Mother who spoke to me. Her voice. That's what I'm going to believe. Now I'm going to get out of her dress and give it back to her.

She goes down the hallway to the bedrooms. Ann looks at Peter.

82

Vi Leave him alone.

Beat.

Ann I should keep an eye on the stew.

She hesitates, goes to Peter, squeezes his shoulder, then leaves for the kitchen.
Vi has picked up the photo Betty had held. She sets it back down.
Peter starts to stand, to follow Ann, when:

Vi Stay in here.

Peter sits back down. Beat.

The ship after yours – the next ship carrying boys and girls to Canada – was torpedoed by the Germans and sank.

Peter I know that.

Vi (*ignoring him*) They wouldn't let anyone – go after that. You were the last. (*Beat.*) We waited a full week wondering what had happened. If it had been your ship. (*Beat.*) We thought then we might have lost you. I even imagined, sitting in the bath, what it would have been like, felt like – to drown. And to float to the bottom of the sea. Like a leaf, I thought, as it falls. We cried ourselves to sleep. (*Beat.*) The first newspaper accounts said that the little boys had stood in perfect lines, all straight, all calm. Some could get into boats, some couldn't. Calm. Betty said that surely meant you couldn't be on that ship, our little Peter couldn't ever stand still. (*She smiles at Peter, then:*) For a week we held our breath. And then we heard. You were in Canada. You were lucky. How we celebrated! Mum and Dad and Betty and Ann and me. How happy we were that our Peter was safe. I'd never known a happier day. (*She picks up the photo again.*) I began to dream you were coming home. (*Beat.*) Then, finally, you really were coming home. (*She sets the photo back down.*) Now you're home. (*She stands. Calls.*) Betty, I'll help you with that dress!

She heads down the hallway. Peter sits alone on the sofa.
   Suddenly, from far off, the distant cry of a baby.
   The cry gets louder and louder, closer and closer. The baby is screaming now.
   Peter doesn't move, doesn't flinch as the baby screams.

SCENE EIGHT

Months later. Midnight.
   The room is dark. Outside – in the hallway – a baby is crying.
   Someone is trying to unlock the door. Finally, it opens and Mike and Ann enter. She carries their crying infant.

Ann (*rocking*) Sh-sh. They're not up. They're asleep. Maybe we should –.

Mike They won't be for long. (*He nods down the hall to the bedrooms.*) Someone's turned on a light.

Ann (*rocking*) Sh-sh. Turn on a lamp.

Mike turns on a lamp. There is a cup and saucer on a table.

Look at this mess. These children need a mother.

Mike It's a cup and saucer.

Betty, tying her dressing gown, enters from the bedrooms.

Betty Ann? Is that you? What are you –?

Vi (*right behind her*) They brought Mary!

84

The aunts go to the child.

Betty What's wrong? Is something wrong?

Ann Sh-sh. Sh-sh.

Mike Colic. I tell her it'll pass. She's worried –.

Ann I'm not worried.

Mike (*over this*) And I'm also her doctor! Give her to them. Give her –. Look at your sisters, they're drooling to –. They won't drop her –.

Ann begins handing over the baby to Betty.

Betty Sh-sh. Sh-sh. She's so sweet.

Vi What time is it?

Mike Midnight.

Vi What are you doing –?

Mike (*to Betty*) We miss you at the surgery.

Betty (*just rocks the baby, ignoring Mike*) God, I love her.

Peter appears in the doorway to Mike and Ann's old bedroom (now his). He has thrown on trousers, and is buttoning his shirt. He is barefoot.

Peter What is – all this?

Mike Peter! (*to Ann*) He is here. You weren't sure –.

Peter Sure what?

Vi Ann's brought Mary.

Mike I'll wager he guessed that.

Peter (*about the crying*) What's wrong?

Ann It's nothing – colic. It goes away. It's a phase, Mike says.

85

Betty Maybe she needs to be changed.

Ann You can try that, sometimes –.

Vi Or she's hungry.

Ann I just fed her.

Mike We brought nappies –.

Betty Let's take her into our room and change her on the bed. (*to Ann*) Do you mind?

Ann I'll have my chances. Please. I hold her enough.

Vi (*to Betty*) Why don't you let me –.

Ann Please, don't fight over her.

Smiles. Vi takes the still-crying baby.
   As the baby is taken out of the room Mike sits on the sofa and sighs:

Mike The lungs on that child. I am so tired.

Soon he will fall asleep sitting up. Ann and Peter look at each other.

Ann I thought you might want to see your niece. You can go – if you want –.

Peter She's beautiful. I'll see more of her later. She's very beautiful.

Big yawn from Mike.

Mike Children . . .

Ann It's not too late –?

Peter No.

Ann You were up?

Peter Yes.

Beat.

Ann You didn't come to the hospital. I don't blame you, they're –. (*Beat. Looks around.*) Our first time out. We just brought her home, you know. She was crying. We couldn't sleep. (*Looks at Mike, who is falling asleep.*) I couldn't sleep. (*Smiles.*) So I thought to myself – where can we go? Who'd take us in? (*Smiles again.*) And I knew you'd be anxious to see her. To meet your niece. I thought you'd been waiting –. It's great to see you.

They look at each other. He reaches for her hand. She resists.

You deserve better than me. You're my brother.

Suddenly, young Rose, Hugh's daughter, comes out from Peter's bedroom, wearing Peter's dressing gown.

Rose Peter?? What's going on? Why is that baby crying?

Ann is stunned to see Rose.

Peter Go back to bed. They'll be gone soon.

Rose Is the baby all right? It's not sick –.

Ann She's fine. They're changing her.

Rose Could I watch? I love babies.

Ann Put some clothes on first.

Rose (*in disbelief*) What??

Ann I said, young lady, put some clothes on first.

Rose looks at Peter, hesitates, then hurries back to put on clothes.

Was that who I think it was?

Peter Rose.

Ann Thank you, I forgot the name. God you people keep secrets.

Peter We just went out for the first time tonight.

Ann I see. (*Beat.*) Good for you. Good for you.

She goes to hug Peter. He hesitates, then allows himself to be hugged.

Though I hope you don't get serious about her. You can do better than that. After all, you're my brother.

This makes Peter smile. Ann sits in a chair. Mike is sound asleep.

It's breezy outside. She'll probably catch a cold. (*Beat.*) What kind of mother am I? (*She turns to Peter for comfort or a compliment.*)

Peter I don't know

Short pause.

Ann When I was in labour, when I was – out. Mike made sure I was out. I had a dream about the baby. I dreamed my baby and I were taking a trip together. Just us. Her and me. We were climbing mountains somewhere. Maybe – Canada? Your mountains?

Peter They're not my –.

Ann The sky was so blue. Her face young and happy. And then suddenly she slipped, Peter, and she started to fall. I reached down and grabbed her hand. I was the only thing keeping her from death. (*Beat.*) She was dangling over the side of a cliff, my hand gripping her wrist. She was so heavy, Peter. I thought my whole arm would fall off. But I held on. (*Beat.*) Then somehow I found the strength, the power inside me, a power that surprised me, that I never knew I possessed, and I pulled my baby to safety. I saved her, Peter. (*Beat.*) I saved her. (*Beat.*) And then there she was again – a baby in my arms. (*Beat.*) You'll adore her. And she'll worship you.

The crying has stopped.

She's stopped crying.

Vi appears.

Vi (*in a loud whisper*) If you sing to her, she stops crying!

Vi hurries back to the baby.
   Off we hear Vi and Betty singing.
   Ann and Peter listen.

Peter What are they singing?

They and we begin to make out the song, 'Goodnight Children Everywhere'.

Vi and Betty (*off*)
   She's with you night and day
   Goodnight children, everywhere.

Mike snores.
   Peter and Ann don't move, can't move, they only listen.

Sleepy little eyes and sleepy little head
Sleepy time is drawing near
In a little while
You'll be tucked up in your bed
Here's a song for baby dear.

Fighting back tears, and without looking at each other, Peter snaps his fingers once – because he is thinking of Mother.
   Ann snaps her fingers once.
   Then after a moment, Ann snaps her fingers twice – she is thinking of Father.

Peter snaps his fingers twice.
The singing continues.
Rose bursts in buttoning her blouse. She crosses the
room and exits to go and see the baby.
Neither seemed to notice her. Off:

Goodnight children, everywhere
Your mummy thinks of you tonight,
Lay your head upon your pillow,
Don't be a kid or a weeping willow.
Close your eyes and say a prayer
And surely you can find a kiss to spare.
Though you are far away
She's with you night and day
Goodnight children, everywhere.